Beyond
the Monkey Bars

Overcoming the Deception of My Formative Years

TROY KANE

12 Publications

12 Publications

ISBN: 978-0-578-14191-6

PRINTED IN THE UNITED STATES OF AMERICA

Disclaimer

This memoir details the true events of the author's difficult childhood and complicated family situation. For legal purposes and to maintain the anonymity of the individuals involved, some characters may have been merged or left out, and character names, places and dates have been changed. The names for health care institutions and agency names have been changed; identification with existing health care institutions and agencies is not intentional. While the conversations are not written to represent the actual word-for-word transcripts, the essence of these conversations is accurate.

Contents

ii

Foreword

Munchausen by Proxy Syndrome (MBPS), also known as Factitious Disorder by Proxy or "fabrication of illness in a child" is a form of child maltreatment that is particularly difficult for healthcare providers to recognize, understand and manage. As in Troy Kane's memoir about his childhood, others, including family members, and especially the spouse of the parent who is fabricating the illness, may also fail to recognize what is going on. While fabrication of illness is most frequently related to physical illness, fabrication can also create symptoms suggesting mental illness. While there are firsthand accounts by victims of MBPS presenting as physical illness in the literature, *Beyond the Monkey Bars* provides an unusual, if not unique, firsthand account of a victim of MBPS suffering from his mother's need to convey that he suffered from mental illness.

Among many important communications, *Beyond the Monkey Bars* serves as a warning that fabrication of illness in MBPS may progress to induction of illness, and even death. It also serves to underscore the fact that in addition to the risk for harm due to invasive medical interventions prompted by MBPS, it may also involve direct emotional and physical abuse of the child by the offending parent, almost always the mother.

But this book is much more than a grim testament to the disturbed thinking and abusive behavior of a very ill mother. It conveys in vivid detail how she was successful for a period of time in persuading even her own son that he was mentally ill with symptoms she had fabricated. His need to identify with her projection of his illness was necessary in order to maintain his attachment to her and the rest of his family. And as with other forms of child maltreatment, the impact was to make the victim, Troy Kane, feel trapped by guilt and shame and unable to speak the truth for many years, as he desperately hoped he could find a way to satisfy his mother and reunite with his family.

Most importantly, *Beyond the Monkey Bars* is a celebration of Troy Kane's remarkable resilience from the adverse impact of years of terrible maltreatment. He describes his journey to achieve remembrance and forgiveness. He emerges from a nightmare of childhood memories to promote four tenets of personal strength and positive mental health: build on things you do well; be persistent; be honest with yourself and don't make excuses; and be positive, not vindictive. Hatred and the desire for vengeance are poison to our souls. Kane's remarkable resilience and the support of others in his life helped him to find a way to overcome his initial feelings of shame and guilt and avoid the subsequent temptation to engage in blame and revenge. His account of his journey is riveting.

Troy Kane's resilience in the face of terrible maltreatment is related in part to his intelligence and capacity for reflection. Moreover, his athletic skill gave him an area of enjoyment and self-esteem that was recognized and supported by others. In addition, he was fortunate to experience other positive, self-affirming attachments as people responded to his friendliness and respect for others. Troy received care in an era when lengthy out of home placements were much more common than today. Ironically, it was his good fortune to have had some longer periods of time to live in settings in which who he really was, a healthy, engaging although shy child, could be validated. Kane's care in the research of his story, including reviewing his mother's journal and obtaining his psychiatric records, provides a meticulously researched account of how the hoax of his mental illness was promulgated and implemented. It underscores how the MBPS parent may be very effective in ingratiating herself and conning medical professionals whose own objectivity may become compromised.

In the penultimate chapter on "Questions, Answers, and Hindsight," Kane acknowledges his own uncertainty about whether his mother's manipulations were conscious decisions or if she was deluding herself, or both—a question that exists for the entire field of medicine, with the only certainty being that parents practicing MBPS on their children can cause enormous mental and physical harm to them, particularly when unsuspecting medical professionals are duped into participation by invasive tests or procedures. Kane also notes that the involvement and oversight of adults who were *not* duped, such as the psychiatrist who provided treatment at the Brantfield Mental Health Institute, and Troy's probation officer from the Youth Development Council, helped to keep his mother's efforts to harm him in some check.

Beyond the Monkey Bars is a remarkable memoir for many reasons. It is a detailed, captivating account of a most unusual growing up that celebrates resilience and recovery over terrible adversity. It provides a rare view of the experience of being the victim of, and ultimately the victor over, a form of child maltreatment that although uncommon, is not rare. It also provides an insider's view of a type of institutional care for children in both the mental health and juvenile justice systems that, mostly for the better, has largely ceased to exist. It helps us to understand how children who are victimized in this way can be coerced into colluding with the abusing parent. This book should be required reading for all pediatric physical and behavioral health care providers, as a reminder to be aware of the potential for the diagnosis of MBPS, particularly when the history reported by the concerned parent does not respond to usual care and cannot be corroborated by other independent observers. And finally, this real life story will inspire anyone who reflects on the innocence of childhood and roots for resilience and a positive outlook to win out.

Peter Metz, MD
Clinical Professor of Psychiatry and Pediatrics
University of Massachusetts Medical School

Introduction

I had an English teacher in high school, Mr. Buxton was his name, and he sometimes had us rewrite our compositions and take an entirely different approach. In the beginning, this really bugged me. If I took the time to write a paper, why did I have to write it again? However, by the end of the school year, I came to appreciate his point that the same story can have different perspectives and be told in a variety of ways.

The core of my story is that I experienced and survived an unusual and traumatic childhood. It was confusing and complex, as my mother was seemingly convinced I was mentally ill and had epileptic seizures that she said caused me to be destructive and violent at home. She said many of these things I did happened in the middle of the night, when my father was at work and my mother and siblings were sleeping. It led to me seeing a series of medical and psychiatric specialists, and spending parts of my youth in a mental institution and juvenile detention centers.

I didn't remember doing the things my mother said I did, but she was so confident I had done them. I was confused, juggling thoughts that there had to be some mistake but at the same time feeling guilty. When I was away in institutions, I never got in any trouble and wanted to go back home to my family. When I was home, my mother severely punished me and I wondered if I would survive.

I have come to believe I was the victim of a mother with Munchausen by Proxy syndrome, which is a highly unusual form of child abuse in which the caregiver, usually the mother, fabricates physical and/or mental illness in the child to gain sympathy and attention for herself, and perhaps satisfaction from fooling the experts. As a young boy, I never considered this was even a possibility.

Eventually, I got through it and got my life back on track, but purposefully guarded this secret past life from friends, coworkers and even some of my own family. I hope that in sharing this story now that it helps health care providers better understand and identify Munchausen by Proxy, and protects children from this harmful deception.

This story isn't about blame; instead it is about persistence, adaptability and rewarded hope that things would get better. As Mr. Buxton might have pointed out, I could have written it differently, and I know that I could have lived it differently, but this story chronicles a difficult beginning that blossoms into a productive adult life.

1
Red Sky in the Morning

Looking at the sunset over Belport beach, Dad used to say:

Red sky at night, sailor's delight,
Red sky in morning, sailors take warning.

There are scientific reasons about weather systems and how the sun's rays, passing at a low angle at sunset and sunrise, light up the underbellies of moisture-rich clouds. In my childhood, the early morning and late night often foretold my fate. On this morning in March, 1964, the morning sky was red.

* * * *

I was lying in bed with my eyes open. Brian and Doug were still sleeping. The three of us slept in the small back bedroom on the second floor. The crumpled, dirty clothes on the floor formed a wall-to-wall rug. We didn't really notice that it was crowded or messy.

I heard the sound of footsteps working their way up the stairs. It was Mom. Instinctively I closed my eyes and pretended to be asleep. She slid the lock on the outside of the bedroom door and opened it. I quickly glanced up.

Mom poked her head into the room and took a deliberate look around. Then she said, "Boys, it's time to get up."

She gently shook Brian to make sure he was awake. Sometimes my older brother Brian struggled to get up for school, but not this morning. Brian was in fourth grade, two years ahead of me. Doug sprung up and hopped out of bed. He went to preschool, but he was going to stay with our neighbor, Mrs. LaFleur, this day. Brian and Doug headed downstairs to get breakfast.

Mom began to walk towards me. By this point, my eyes were wide open and I no longer pretended to be sleepy. Like so many other mornings, I worried that she would start asking questions that I couldn't answer and then punish me. Dad wasn't home yet from the donut shop. He worked six nights a week making donuts and muffins in run-down Elkon Square. I tried to stay calm, but my heart was pounding as she approached. I glanced up at her face and tried to read her mood, but I got no clues.

Finally, she reached towards me and I felt panicked, but I tried to look relaxed. She said, "Troy, we've got a busy day ahead of us. You better hurry up and have your breakfast."

I took a deep breath. Before she could change her mind, I replied, "Okay."

Mom untied the restraints on my wrists and ankles. To keep me from getting out of bed in the middle of the night, she wrapped nylon stockings around my wrists and ankles and tied them securely to the bed.

I hated it. It made me feel like a criminal. I had to sleep on my back and it hurt if I tried to move. I didn't dare complain. Mom also had Dad nail the only window in the bedroom shut so I wouldn't crawl out on the roof, and put the small, slide bolt lock on the outside of the bedroom door to prevent me from wandering at night.

I started to get up; my sheets and pajamas were wet. I quickly washed up, got changed and went downstairs. My sister, Robin, five years older than me, was sitting at the kitchen table, which was actually a wooden picnic table with a red and white plastic tablecloth and two long benches. Brian and Doug were sitting on one of the benches, eating their breakfast. I got some corn flakes, took my seat next to Robin and looked at the back of the cereal box as I ate. There was an offer for a plastic model of the atomic submarine, USS Nautilus, which said it was the first sub to travel under the icy North Pole. The cost was a quarter and two box tops. The picture was neat, but I couldn't help but imagine getting stuck under the ice and not being able to breathe.

We didn't say much to each other, but it was obvious that we all felt sad and unnerved. I didn't know when I would be sitting at the kitchen table with them again.

Robin was in the seventh grade and went to the Belport Junior High in the center of town. She had a long walk ahead of her and had to get going or she would be late. As the oldest kid in our family, she understood better than my brothers what to expect. Robin looked out for me, but there wasn't anything she could do this day. Tears flowed down her cheeks as she hugged me.

"We'll come visit you as soon as we can. I'll miss you," she said.

I wiped away my tears and muttered back that I would miss her, too. Robin hurried out the door. Brian gave me a pat on the back and said goodbye. Brian was on his way to the Roosevelt School, about a half-mile uphill walk along Atlantic Boulevard and the beach. It was high tide and the waves were breaking over the top of the wall. Sometimes on our way to school, we ran along the edge of the wall and tried not to get wet as the relentless waves crashed against the rocks and sand. If a wave was going to hit you, you stood like a flamingo with one leg up and one on the sand and rocks. This way, only one shoe got soaked by the salty water. Sometimes when a big wave rolled up, I forgot which leg was the dry one and ended up with both shoes and pant legs soaked.

3

Not too long after Brian left, Dad came home from work. Mom didn't like it that Dad worked nights. When we lived in Powell, he used to work an early day shift and was back home in the afternoon. Sometimes he even came home for lunch. Dad had changed jobs a few times over the last few years, working 70 to 80 hours per week at times, to pay for my medical bills.

Having your father work in a donut shop had its advantages. On Saturdays, Dad usually brought home fresh donuts for us. My favorite was a white-powdered donut with lemon filling. He smiled at me and gave me a quick hug. I always felt safe and more relaxed when Dad was home.

Mom said, "Russ, I'm going to take Doug to Edith's."

Edith LaFleur's husband was the head Maitre D' at a fancy French restaurant in Mason Heights. They both had strong accents, having relocated from France. Edith gave us fruit and snacks when we went to the beach with her family. Sometimes she yelled at her kids when they didn't listen to her, but she was always nice to me.

As we waited for Mom to get back, Dad said, "I heard a new joke. You want to hear it?

"Sure."

"What is black and white and red all over?"

I remembered he told us this joke last week. "It's a newspaper," I answered.

He smiled and said, "No, it's a zebra with a rash."

We both laughed. Sometimes, after supper, Dad told jokes or funny stories about when he was a kid. Since Dad worked nights, he went back to bed after supper for a few hours before going to work. Sometimes we asked him to tell us the same story over and over, because we didn't want him to go to bed. I didn't always get Dad's jokes, but I loved the way he told them and I loved to laugh with him. Sometimes, he teased Mom because a lot of times she didn't understand his jokes either, or she started laughing way after the joke was over.

Mom got back a few minutes later and it was just about time for us to go.

She suggested to me, "Why don't you check to make sure you have everything?"

I pushed the metal tabs on my new little blue suitcase, and the hinge sprung open. "Ya. I have everything."

I put my toothpaste and toothbrush in the corner of the suitcase. Then I folded my PJs again and placed them back in, and grabbed Buddy, my stuffed animal bear. I had a lot of stuffed animals, but Buddy was my favorite. Mom said I couldn't bring a lot of things with me.

It was time to go. As we walked out the door, the smell of the ocean air was strong and the wind was blowing hard. The metal sign on our front lawn, with our name, *The Kanes*, spelled out on it, was rattling. Mom shielded me from the wind as we hurried to the car.

I sat in the front seat between Mom and Dad. Usually, Doug sat there because he was the youngest. Dad was quiet as we drove along the beach and headed towards Mason Heights. One by one, the waves crashed against the wall. The biggest ones splashed over the top. I was going to miss the beach. Mom put her arm around me and started to sing a familiar, hopeful song, Look for the Silver Lining.

As Mom sang the high part, Dad kicked in with the harmony. I hummed along with the melody. For the moment, I felt safe and warm.

After the song, Mom sat up straighter and looked me in the eye.

"Troy, I want you to understand that this is the only way we can get you the treatment you need. You know I love you."

Mom had explained this to me a bunch of times. I knew she was doing everything she could to get me better. But I didn't want to go to court and I didn't want to live somewhere else. I wanted to stay home.

"I know," I said nervously, because I didn't know what would happen or where I would end up.

2
The Early Years

On September 7, 1812, French forces, led by Napoleon, and Russian soldiers, led by General Kutozov, met 75 miles west of Moscow in an epic battle. Napoleon's Grande Armée had defeated much of Europe and had successfully fought its way deep into Russian territory. With the balance of Moscow and the nation riding on their efforts, the Russian army fought bitterly, with a combined total of 70,000 soldiers from the two sides dying. This battle ignited a series of losses and retreats on the battlefield for Napoleon, extending into the cold winter, which ultimately led to Napoleon's defeat. In 1880, Tchaikovsky was commissioned to write a song to commemorate that proud stand for Russian freedom. Two years later, Tchaikovsky's 1812 Overture debuted at the Moscow Exhibition. In his composition, he captured the emotion of the tumultuous battle, with its series of quick-paced attacks and counterattacks, concluding with the final, dramatic moment of victory.

* * * *

When my parents married, my father was 25 years old and my mother just 21. For the first six months, they lived with my father's family, but then my mother got pregnant. They looked around the area for an apartment and found a place of their own on Omni

Street in the next town over, Powell. The house was a brown, two-decker, with the available two-bedroom apartment on the first floor. There were empty gun shells scattered on the edge of the road from the gun club that was situated towards the bottom of the street. The tall chain-link fence at the bottom of Omni formed the boundary between the high school football field and the dead end street, which was populated with mostly, two-family houses on the right. Sal and Rosa Russo, an older couple that spoke with strong Italian accents, owned the property. When my parents first moved in, Mr. Ferrell lived in the top apartment. He was a cook, and showed my mother how to cook her first turkey. By the time I was born, Sal and Rosa, who we called Uncle Sal and Aunty Rosa, had moved in upstairs. In the morning, you could smell Auntie Rosa's fresh-ground coffee permeating the pores of the house. There was a nice yard for us to play in. Sal kept his two, medium-sized dogs penned up in the back yard.

It was tough for Dad's family when he and Mom moved out on their own. Dad had helped support his family since he was just eight years old; his first job was getting up early in the morning to deliver newspapers to 300 customers before he went to school. Now, Dad worked as the baker at Mrs. Pond's donut shop in downtown Powell. Mom worked there, too, bringing hot coffee and donuts, and light sandwiches at lunch to the steady stream of customers that drifted in from the bustling street.

With their first baby on the way and an apartment to pay for, Dad became focused on his own family. Dad's mother, who we came to call Grammie, was one of 12 kids in her family. When Grammie was growing up, her father routinely worked at the post office and other part-time jobs to make enough to pay for expenses for his large family. Grammie was a small, attractive woman who was lame and had a pronounced limp. She had a quiet determination and always found a way to do what she had to do.

A few months after my parents moved into their apartment, my mother gave birth to Robin. For the first eight years of marriage, my mother was pregnant a lot of the time. We ended up with four kids in our family, although my mother also had a few miscarriages. My brother, Brian, followed Robin in the birth order. He was named after Dad's father, Brian Earl Kane, who had died earlier in the year.

With my grandfather's resemblance to baseball hero Babe Ruth, some people called him Babe. He had seven sisters and no brothers, and became accustomed to being pampered. He had a good sense of humor and could be quite charming. When Dad was born, Babe carried him throughout the nursery area in the hospital boasting to anyone within shouting distance, "This is what a baby should look like!" Although he was a talented carpenter, for some reason he often didn't work.

I was the third kid, followed by Doug who came along two years after me to round out the family.

When I was two years old, Uncle Sal set up a ladder in the back yard so he could do some work on the upper part of the house. It was a warm day, and after working for awhile he climbed down the ladder and went into the house, probably to get a cool drink and rest for a few minutes.

Something about that ladder caught my eye. I walked over to it, leaned forward and gripped the rung that was about chest high on me with both hands. Then I put my right foot on the first rung, and stepped up with my left foot. I was on the ladder. I reached up with my right hand and hooked the next rung, followed by a step up with my right foot. I quickly developed a rhythm and made my way up the ladder.

Mom was in the kitchen doing the dishes and saw my little feet scaling the ladder through the window overlooking the back yard.

She called out, "Troy."

She walked briskly out the back door. She saw the angled ladder, following its lines up to the second floor level, where I was now perched.

Mom took a deep breath and in a calm voice, said, "Troy .... Come on down, honey."

"Hi, Mom," I said proudly.

"Troy. Be careful and come down the ladder, nice and slow," she said.

I smiled. After a little more coaxing, I started to come down, slowly at first.

"Okay. Good. Hold on tight. Keep coming," she said in a slow, melodic tone.

Again, it started to flow naturally as I made my way down quickly, oblivious to the inherent danger.

"Be careful. .... That's good, Troy."

When I got within reach, Mom anxiously grabbed me around the waist and pulled me close to her.

"Don't you ever do that again!" she yelled, relieved and angry at the same instant.

My pride turned to tears, as she began spanking me.

"You scared me half to death. Don't ever do that again!"

As a two-year old, I generally did what my mother said, and usually didn't get in much trouble. But Mom had a bad temper, and all of us would get it from her sometimes. I don't know why, but somewhere along the way, things started to get worse for me.

Mom brought me to see Dr. Duffy, our pediatrician.

"You said on the phone that Troy is having some problems. What is happening?" he asked.

"Well, I wasn't sure the first time it happened, but Troy has been blacking out sometimes. He gets very stubborn and angry when he is scolded, and sometimes he holds his breath. It's very upsetting because I don't know if he is going to breathe again. A few times, he has blacked out entirely."

"Well, Mrs. Kane, I will check him out thoroughly, but kids sometimes hold their breath and do other things to get their parents' attention," said Dr. Duffy.

After he completed examining me, Dr. Duffy said, "All of Troy's signs are good, so there isn't anything physically wrong with him. I know it is hard to watch your son holding his breath like that, but the best thing to do is ignore him when he does it. Once he learns that you're not going to react to what he is doing, he will stop holding his breath."

"Well, he sure looked like he was in danger, but I'll try what you say," said Mom.

"Now, you listen to your mother and behave yourself, Troy," said Dr. Duffy as he shuffled us out of the examining room.

Dad punished us if we did something wrong, but Mom kept an eye on everything, and was stricter. Brian had a habit of writing the letter B for Brian in any unblemished dust he found in the house. Still learning to write his letters, Brian distinctively wrote his Bs backwards, so it was easy for Mom to know who did it and punish him. He had a temper, not as bad as Mom's, but sometimes he was tough on Robin and me. Brian's signature B was not lost on Robin, who when she wanted to get Brian back, left perfect counterfeit Bs, which got him punished by Mom and made him even angrier for getting in trouble for something he didn't do.

Mom was not able to solve all the mysteries of the house. When something was out of sorts, she would ask us questions to get to the bottom of things. Mom would find tricky ways to word her questions, maybe adding "not" to change the meaning and throw us off. She pushed for answers to her questions, and they had to be the right answers. Sooner or later, she would get us to admit to what we did, even if we didn't do it. Once you said you did something, you couldn't take it back. You were guilty.

I started to get punished more and more as time went on,

sometimes severely. When Mom got mad, you had better watch out. If I held my breath in protest, Mom would stick me with a pin. I sometimes asked her to let Dad punish me when he got home from work. Dad wasn't mean. Sometimes, I thought about running away from her.

After one time when I admitted to something I didn't do and was punished, I threatened, "I'm going to run away."

I sat at the kitchen table, still angry and hugging Buddy, my stuffed bear. Dad hadn't come home from work yet. Mom noticed my paper bag filled with neatly folded clothes, a few toys and my tooth brush.

"I thought you were running away," Mom said nonchalantly.

"I am. I'm waiting for Dad to drive me," I said defiantly.

I didn't have a plan of where I would go, or what I would do when I got there, or how long I would stay, but I was mad.

I felt more comfortable when Dad was around, but he went in early to work at the donut shop six days a week to make fresh do-nuts, muffins and pastry for the morning rush. Sometimes he would come home for lunch, before returning to finish his day. When Dad slowly turned down Omni Street and parked his black, two-door Chevy in front, my mood picked up.

"I made you a baloney sandwich. Do you want some chocolate milk with it?" Mom asked Dad.

"No. I'll just have regular milk."

"I'll have choclit!" said Brian.

"Me too," said Robin.

"Me too," I chimed in.

We quickly ate our peanut butter and jelly sandwiches. Dad told us a few jokes and we all laughed. Then Mom and Dad talked some more about the store and grown-up things.

"I have a lot to do so I better get back to work," said Dad, push-ing his chair back from the table.

Immediately, Robin and Brian jumped up from the table.

Robin hurriedly waved her hands at me and said, "Come on!"

"Oh ya," I remembered.

I jumped out of my chair and rushed to the front door with them.

Robin pulled hard and swung open the big car door. With the car parked on a slight hill, once the door started going, there was no stopping it. She pushed Mom's seat forward. Brian crawled in first, then me. Robin got in and pulled the seat back in place and managed to shut the car door. We hid on the floor, waiting.

After a moment, I asked, "Is he coming yet?"

Brian put his index finger over his mouth. "SSHHH! Quiet."

We waited for another few minutes. We were giggling.

"Is he coming?" I asked again.

Whack went the screen door as the spring pulled it shut, and Dad and Mom came out on the piazza.

"He's coming!" said Brian in a hushed voice.

"SHHH," Robin said.

"Well, Brenda, I better get back to work. I wanted to kiss the kids goodbye, but I'm in a hurry. Tell them I'll see them when I get home," said Dad loudly.

I started to giggle. Just like when Mom told us to stop laughing at church, I couldn't help myself. Robin and Brian were giggling too, but they quieted down quickly. I put both my hands over my mouth to hold back the flood of laughter that wanted to escape.

Dad kissed Mom. Then he opened the car door and got in. He hesitated, then said, "Brenda, did you hear something?"

We all tried really hard, but the laughing noises were escaping like air rushing from untied balloons. I tucked my head into my knees, hoping Dad wouldn't notice me.

"What *was* that?" Dad asked.

This time he turned around and looked towards the back seat.

He reached his hand out, feeling blindly in the air. I ducked lower, kept one hand over my mouth and breathed through my nose. *He didn't see us!*

"Okay, Brenda. I'll see you later." He fumbled loudly with the keys and then started up the engine.

VAROOM! I couldn't hold it back any longer. I laughed loudly. Brian and Robin did, too!

"Hey, what are you kids doing in the car?" asked Dad.

"We fooled you!" Brian called out.

"Ya. We fooled you!" I repeated.

Broadly smiling, Dad said, "Okay. You better get out so I can get back to work."

Mom was smiling too. We crawled out of the car and waved as Dad headed back to work.

When Dad finished work for the day, a lot of times he came home and played with us. My favorite was when we played baseball. We all got a chance to hit the ball and catch it. When I got up, Dad told me to pick up the bat, hold it back and off my shoulder. And be sure to keep my eye on the ball. When he pitched it, I swung as hard as I could, but I missed it a lot.

When Brian threw the ball back to Dad, it went right into the ground. This happened a few more times.

"Brian, look up when you throw the ball," Dad instructed patiently.

Dad held the ball in his right hand, and held his chin up, looking straight ahead at me and Brian. With perfect form, he bent his elbow, then straightened it and released the ball.

I swung and missed again. Brian picked it up and threw it back into the ground a few feet in front of the plate.

"Brian, look at me and throw up," Dad instructed.

Well, three little kids never laughed harder.

Brian said, "Throw up. Dad said throw up."

Dad laughed with us. It took a few minutes to settle down.

Dad said I had a good swing. He helped me hold the bat the right way, and eventually I started to hit the ball. I batted lefty and so did Robin. Brian was a lefty, but he batted righty. Dad never told us which way to stand, he let us bat whatever way we wanted.

Even at a young age, I already loved baseball. One of the best things was going to watch Dad play fast-pitch softball at night. He played third base and was busy in the action with all the bunting and stealing. When Dad got up to bat, he had his own cheering section, with Mom leading Robin, Brian, me and now Doug with choruses of, "We want a hit! We want a hit!"

One game, he got up in the last inning with two outs. His team was down by one run, but they had guys on second and third. Dad smacked a line drive between the outfielders and it rolled a long way. He ran hard to first base as his teammates scored the winning runs. We all yelled as his team mobbed him. I couldn't help think that he ran so fast in his softball games, but he couldn't run fast enough to beat me in our races.

When we got home from a game, it was after my bedtime. So I got ready for bed as fast as I could. I hummed the 1812 Overture.

ta-da, ta-da, ta-da, ta-da
ta-da, ta-da, ta-da, ta-da
ta-da, ta-da, ta-da, ta-da
ta-daaaa, ta-da, ta-daaa.

While humming, I quickly folded my clothes and put them in a neat pile. I placed my sneakers evenly side-by-side just under the edge of my bed. I put on my PJs, pulled back the covers and quickly hopped into bed, finishing proudly with a crescendo leading to:

ta-da, ta-da, ta-daaaaaaa.

Even though I got mad at her sometimes, I still liked to spend time with Mom too. I remember a rainy day with Mom that was special. She decided to make donuts. Mom mixed the dough, and then rolled it out on the kitchen table. She sprinkled flour on the top and then let me cut out some of the donuts, just like we watched Dad do at work sometimes. As we made the donuts, the storm grew worse. The strong winds pushed the branches on the tree in the back yard back and then forth, until finally the big tree snapped from the hurricane-force winds. I felt the thump as the biggest limb hit the ground and shook the floor in the kitchen. The thick branch stretched across the yard pointing towards us, but it didn't reach the house. I was startled and scared. So was Mom. She pulled me close and hugged me.

Although Robin and Brian helped make the donuts that day, too, it felt like it was just Mom and me.

"You're the best Mom in the whole world," I said.

The smell of donuts lasted the entire day.

* * * *

In September of 1959, Dad changed jobs and started working at Cromona's Bakery. Maybe Dad and Mom needed more money, because Dad worked long hours then. He was still a baker, but they had a lot of bakers working there. He made bread and cakes and pastries. Dad worked all night and some of the morning too. He had to go to sleep during part of the day, so we didn't get to see him as much. Sometimes he didn't get any days off for weeks at a time.

It wasn't as much fun as before. And I don't think Mom liked it either, because she seemed to get angry about a lot of things, like keeping the house clean. If I spilled milk on the kitchen floor or Brian or Robin did, we had to watch out. She yelled at us and sometimes spanked whoever did it; then she cried and cried as she sopped up the milk. She also noticed scrapes in the wallpaper, scratches in the woodwork and crayon marks on the floor. She sure was mad.

Mom also started asking more questions, especially about me.

On Christmas day, Mom asked, "Robin, you were in the parlor. Did you notice Troy talking to himself?"

"No Mom. I didn't," answered Robin.

Mom turned to Brian and said, "You must have Brian."

"No Mom," he said.

"Well, you were in the parlor with Troy, right?"

"Um ... ya."

".... when he was talking to himself," she finished.

"No, he didn't say anything," explained Brian.

Mom got angrier. It took a while longer and a lot more questions, but Brian finally agreed that maybe I had been talking a little to myself.

I was about four years old at that point, and Mom was worried that I was having problems mentally. She started reading Sigmund Freud books. She read passages of the books to then nine year-old Robin, and asked her if the problems Freud described sounded like me.

Mom had some of her own health problems to deal with, and went to the hospital to have her appendix removed. Not long after she recovered from the surgery and came home, she immediately became upset and began clearing out the food in the kitchen.

"Troy poisoned the food. We have to throw it all away so no one else gets sick," she said.

Mom emptied the kitchen of practically any food that was open or could have been compromised. She was not going to take any chances. I didn't know why she blamed me. I didn't do anything to the food. It was an awful feeling being the one who was responsible. Even though I didn't taint the food, it felt like I had done it.

By the summer, I was constantly worried about getting in trouble, and the situation continued to get worse. Mom often asked me in the morning, "Troy, were you up again during the middle of the night?"

I felt scared. I was afraid to answer her because whatever I said could quickly become the proof she was looking for.

"No Mom," I mumbled softly.

"Well, what happened to the window sill in the parlor? It's all scraped. Did *you* do that?"

"No," I said nervously.

"Well, then how did it happen?" she continued.

"I, um, I don't know," I stammered, searching my mind for a quick answer, but more and more feeling resigned to being in trouble.

She asked me a few more things, but didn't get anything out of me. I didn't know if it was good not to give her answers or make some things up and get caught in a lie, but she got mad when I didn't say anything. With anger and frustration showing in her eyes, she reached and grabbed me. In one motion, she turned me and slapped the back of my legs as I put my hands behind me to shield myself. It was no use. She pulled my hands away.

"I'm sorry. I didn't mean it," I begged.

It was too late. She spanked me harder, her hands flailing and timed with her forewarnings. I stopped trying to get away because it only made her swing harder and for longer. When she finally stopped, I pulled myself together and crawled onto my bed.

Mom was determined to get to the bottom of my problems. She continued to read Freud and took notes about important things she read about, like schizophrenia, anxiety, depression and hallucinations. She also started keeping detailed notes on what I did in the day and at night.

The interrogations and punishments continued. Many days began with, "What did you do last night, Troy?"

The hard part was that she already knew the answer. I didn't remember doing anything and no matter how hard I tried, I couldn't come up with anything that satisfied Mom. Some of it happened at night when everyone was sleeping. Sometimes, Mom stayed up late to try to catch me in the act, and occasionally had Robin join her, but they never caught me doing anything. But that didn't stop her from asking and asking what I had done, and accusing me. She got really mad. Sometimes I made something up so I could just say something to hopefully appease her. But my answers were never good. I cried. Questions and punishment, questions and punishment; the cyclone intensified.

The week before Christmas, Mom got sick again. She said she was having trouble with her heart. She didn't have any strength. I was worried about her; we all were. She hoped she'd feel better with some rest, but two weeks later she was still feeling sick and was admitted to the hospital.

As she said goodbye to all of us before Dad drove her to the hospital, Mom looked tired.

I was worried and I said to her sadly, "I hope you don't die."

Grandma and Mom didn't always get along well, but for the week that Mom spent in the hospital, Grandma helped take care of us. Grandma didn't cook supper or clean the house. Dad did that and worked too, but Grandma was nice to us.

A few weeks after Mom returned from the hospital, things settled down. But in April, Brian got the measles. To prevent it from spreading, Robin, Doug and I got vaccinated. Maybe as a reaction to the shot, I had a fever of 103 degrees for three or four days, and didn't run around like I usually did. I guess I didn't get the measles though, or at least a full-blown case of it, because Mom said I didn't get the rash. She would always make a big deal out of this measles thing, and tell the new doctors what had happened when we first met them.

After the measles shot, things picked up where they left off. Mom was busy jotting things down in her notebook about me. One day she wrote, "He was irritable, impatient, destructive. At times, extremely active—other times, day dreaming and poor behavior seemed to increase daily. "

The next day she wrote, "[Troy] became quiet, depressed, irritable, destructive, and finally hallucinating."

Mom had to do something about it and called Dr. Duffy at his home in a panic at 5:30 one morning, and woke him up. She said I had become very destructive, and I was hallucinating and out of control. She wanted him to give me something that would calm me down, and even suggested getting me admitted to a mental institution. The doctor was noticeably irritated getting roused out of bed so early in the morning. He suggested that Mom call him later in the day at his office, and he would suggest a psychiatrist.

3
What's Wrong with Troy?

Mad Magazine called 1961 an "upside-up year", meaning the numbers look the same if they are turned upside down or appear upside up. They noted it was the first time this had happened since 1881 and it wouldn't happen again until 6009. Not surprisingly, the headline on the magazine predicted it would be a mad year.

* * * *

Brian and I fought sometimes and I thought he was a bully. Mom didn't like our fighting, and we would both get in trouble. I figured Brian had been doing the stuff that Mom said I did, because I didn't do it and I figured Robin didn't. Who else could it be?

Mom said she thought that I had tried to hit Brian with a baseball bat. I got mad at Brian sometimes, but I wouldn't do that. Brian was bigger and stronger than me, and wouldn't let me do something like that anyway. Mom kept asking me about it and about me wanting to hurt my family.

She would get really mad at me. I was scared, and confused. She wanted to know if there was something making me do these things. I didn't think I was doing them. Maybe someone else was doing these things or making me do them, but I didn't think I was. Whatever was happening, I wanted more than anything for it to stop. But I didn't know how to stop it.

I spent a lot time thinking about everything that was happening. What if I really was wrecking things? What if I did try to hurt Brian or Doug? What if I did swing a bat at Brian and hit him?

Each day there were more things. Mom said Brian told her I was going to jump off the scoreboard at the football field and try to kill myself. She said Brian said he talked me out of it. I didn't remember that. Why would Brian say that? Did this really happen?

Then Mom started asking questions about me hearing voices. Was I hearing voices? Did the voices tell me to do things? Did I talk to them? Mom said that sometimes I talked to myself. She wanted to know if I saw who was saying these things to me. I just wanted her to stop asking me about everything. It was worse when Dad was at work or sleeping. But she kept asking me over and over again, and punishing me for things she said I did. I tried hard not to get her angry. I was careful what I said. Sometimes she had that look on her face, her dark brown eyes piercing right through me. I knew what was coming.

"No, Mom. I'm sorry. I'm sorry!"

"This .... is .... what .... happens .... when .... you ..... lie," she said as she took short, choppy breaths between her frantic slaps.

At first, I tried to twist and squirm away from her, but it didn't work and angered her into a blitzkrieg of strikes landing all over me. I just wanted to run out of the room, out the front door and keep running and running away from her and never come back. But I wasn't going anywhere. I couldn't leave the room until her face softened, and the storm cleared. Sometimes that was it, but a lot of times it was just a temporary truce.

"Okay, Troy. Let's start again," she said in a calm tone. "Tell me what you did ...."

There wasn't much else I could say. I had already given her my best answers and they didn't work. I knew I was in big trouble. Panic set in. Silently in my mind I tried as hard as I could to come up with something that would make her say, "Okay, Troy. It's all right."

I knew I didn't have more than a few seconds. Hurry, hurry! But I couldn't come up with the magic answer. I never could. The whirlwind returned, my answers sounding like the others I gave her earlier. The questions came faster and faster. The panic in my face showed I knew the time bomb was ticking. She couldn't hold herself back any longer. Her emotion traveled from the anger in her eyes, into her arms and through her fingers like a burst faucet. She grabbed me in an instant, holding me down and swinging until all her emotion was drained. Then it was finally over, leaving me sobbing and feeling humiliated.

Mom's written notes in her notebook documented how everything was spiraling out of control.

June 9 (Mom's notebook)

Troy slept on the edge of bed so as not to fall thru "hole" in center of mattress. Insisted it was no dream. Told me of hearing voices all the time. They laughed at him—tell him to hit, hurt, kill. Laugh when he gets punished. Said he sees voices, are little devils, hurt him with pitch fork—make him say "yes sir". He has frequent temper tantrums.

Mom didn't know any psychiatrists, but she started looking through the phone book and making calls. First, she tried the State House and the Department of Mental Health. She told them about me being destructive to the house, holding my breath until I turned blue, my reaction to the measles shot, and my hearing voices that told me to hurt my family. They couldn't help, but they told Mom to call Evans Development Center.

So Mom called Evans Development Center and asked them if they could set up counseling for me. Mom told the agonizing story to the social worker all over again. He took down what she said and told her he would tell the psychiatrist about me. But there was a long waiting list there too, and she probably wouldn't hear back for three or four weeks.

June 10 (Mom's notebook)

More writing on woodwork, tore upholstery on kitchen chair. Urinated on bathroom floor—gets mouthful of water and spits it all over house. Said faces come out of wallpaper, laugh at him, boss him. Other faces come out of furniture, light, ceiling, floor. Said voices told him to hit Brian with baseball bat. Bit hole in tube of toothpaste, tube of Unguentine. Says voices whisper to him all the time—wish "they" would leave him alone. Telling him to kill everyone in family but Doug—wait til he grows up. Told me he had climbed to top of scoreboard at football field—was going to dive head first—Brian talked him out of it (Brian verified). Voices told him to jump from top of swing. "They" get in his food. (He is eating poorly).

Mom called Freeman's Children Center and told them about what had been going on, that it was getting worse and more dangerous for the whole family. They said I needed to be hospitalized to find out what was wrong with me, but they couldn't help us.

June 11 (Mom's notebook)

Voices want him dead—tell him to run in front of car. I'm afraid to let him out alone—all his

food "smells" awful. Banged heads with Doug—
later banged his head on windowsill. I noticed
letter T on his foot—said voices told him to write
his name on his feet so they'd know they were
talking to the right kid. Behaves terribly when
Russ is home—punching, yelling, hitting. Jumps
incessantly from steps, chairs, porch railing, etc.

Very overactive. Throwing self against the wall.
Kicked Doug—bit toothpaste tube—not eating at
all—very grouchy. Killed ant "so it could be in
heaven". Kicked his leg into cement wall. Stuck
Doug with pin. Scraped woodwork in pantry, my
room, his bedroom, bathroom, kitchen. Asked if
he was really Troy, wasn't sure.

She continued to look for help. She called the McCauley Clinic, an affiliate of Cavanaugh Medical School. She barely had a chance to tell them about the problem when she learned that they only dealt with teenagers.

Next Mom called the Catholic Charities and they told her to call Grandview Project in Mason Heights. They felt bad for Mom, but told her they handled only outpatient cases. They also had a long waiting list, and told her to bring me to our family doctor. Mom had already tried him.

So Mom called the National Organization for Mentally Ill Children. They offered more sympathy and some things to read that might help her understand what was going on with me a little better, but pointed Mom to Slater County Medical Center to get psychiatric testing for me.

Mom called the Children's Psychiatric Division at Slater County Medical Center, but they didn't have any psychiatrists on duty during the weekend. They told her to call back Monday.

Mom kept trying and it finally paid off. She called Mason Heights Children's Center and explained about the destruction I caused, the voices that told me to do things like hitting my brother with a baseball bat, my almost diving off the high school football scoreboard, and my looking off into space sometimes. They agreed with Mom that I might need to be hospitalized, but just like Slater County, they didn't have a psychiatrist on duty during the weekend. But, they did set up an appointment for eight in the morning on Monday, and they said they could admit me right away if necessary.

Early in the morning on June 12, 1961, Dad got out of work early to drive us to Mason Heights. Grandma stayed home with Robin, Brian and Doug. When we got to the front desk at Children's Center, Mom did all the talking while Dad and I stood by. We had to wait a long time before they finally called my name. We went into the doctor's office. He had dark hair and thick glasses. He was taller than Dad. He smiled and seemed nice.

"Hello, my name is Dr. Drake. I am a psychiatrist on the staff here at Children's Center. Let's see, your name is ... Troy?" he asked.

"Yes," I said quietly.

"How old are you, Troy?"

"I'm almost five," I mumbled.

"Well Troy. First I'm going to examine you to make sure you are healthy. Can you take off your shirt and pants and shoes and socks for me?"

I got undressed, folded my clothes in a neat pile, and put them on top of my shoes.

"Well, that was quick," he said.

"He does that at home while humming the 1812 overture... ta da, ta da, ta da, da da. He gets ready for bed faster than any of our kids," Mom said while moving her hands like a conductor of the orchestra.

I let out a little smile.

Dr. Drake did what Dr. Duffy did. He listened to my heart, tucking the black knobs into his ears and placing the cold, round silver part on my chest. My heart was beating fast.

"That sounds really strong," he said.

Then he wrapped a big black thing around my arm and squeezed the black rubber ball hanging from it. It quickly filled with air and squeezed hard against my arm.

"That's good, Troy," he said as he released the air and freed my arm.

He made me stick out my tongue, say ahhhh and looked down my throat.

I thought about Dad's funny story when he was a kid and went to the doctor. Dad's cousin told him that no matter what, don't let the doctor put that little stick he has in your mouth. He said the doctor would push it down his throat and tear out Dad's tonsils. He told Dad that when the doctor tells him to open his mouth and say ahhhh, that was when he was going to do it. Dad did everything the doctor wanted until he told him he wanted to look down his throat.

"This won't hurt a bit. Just open your mouth and say ahhhh," the doctor had said to Dad.

Well, Dad knew better than that. He pulled away from the surprised doctor and ran right out the door and just kept on going.

Now the doctor asked me to touch his finger and then touch my nose, and touch his finger and touch my nose. He kept moving his finger around to make it harder, but I did it every time.

"Troy, you look like an athlete to me. Do you play ball?" he asked.

"Ya."

"What is your favorite sport?"

"Baseball."

"I'll bet you're a good player," he said and smiled at me.

Dad said, "He's got a really good eye at the plate."

"I bet you do. You can get dressed now, Troy," the doctor said.

I wished I was playing ball in the backyard instead of seeing the doctor. I put my clothes on and sat with Mom and Dad.

"Well, there seems to be some troubles at home with Troy and his brothers and sister. Maybe you could tell me about it," he said, looking at Mom and Dad.

Mom began telling him all about me. She started when I was a baby. When I learned to walk and talk. When I stopped wearing diapers. When I started holding my breath until I turned blue. When I got sick from the measles shot.

Then she started to tell him the other stuff. I didn't want her to.

"Troy has always been a very active child, but starting last fall, he would just sit at the kitchen table for hours and didn't want to go out and play. Sometimes, he would turn on the TV, but wouldn't really be watching it. He'd be just staring off into space, like he was daydreaming, but for a long time. He has been getting in fights with his brothers, which all kids do but he does things and then blames them for it. After awhile, he usually admits what he did. He has been very destructive around the house, tearing the wallpaper, and scraping the floors. It's the same thing with him blaming his siblings for it."

The more Mom talked, the more it upset her. She couldn't hold back her tears any longer and had to stop for a minute.

"I'm sorry," said Mom to the doctor. "I just want Troy to be okay, and for the whole family to be happy again."

Mom took a deep sigh and stopped crying. Then said it was hard to raise a family with me doing all these things, and with Dad working a lot and not around as much to help.

Then she started telling him about how things got a lot worse in the past year, when I started hearing voices. She said how I told her the voices were telling me what to do, and that sometimes they laughed at me. As Mom continued, she sniffled here and there but held back her tears.

I felt like I was a bad kid. I was sure the doctor didn't like me. My cheeks and ears felt warm.

The doctor asked Mom some questions, and then asked me and Dad some, too. I didn't have a lot to say. Dad didn't either.

Then the doctor said that they wanted me to stay there for awhile so they could do some tests and try to help me. Mom had some questions for him. She wanted to know if he would be the doctor seeing me and what some of the tests were that they would do.

I hadn't thought about staying at the hospital before then, just that Mom had wanted me to see a doctor. Now I realized Mom and Dad were going home and I was going to be by myself. I didn't want to stay there. I wanted to go home. If Mom gave me another chance, I knew I would be good, but Mom and Dr. Drake had made up their minds.

Before I knew it, I was saying goodbye.

"Don't worry, Troy," Mom said. "They have the best doctors in the world here. They will help you and we will come to visit you soon."

Dad rubbed his hand on the light brown bristles of my crew cut.

"Be a good boy, Troy," he said. "We'll see you soon."

"Tell Robin, Brian and Doug I miss them," I said.

My chin started to quiver as they walked down the hall.

* * * *

Everyone was nice to me at Children's Center. I met other doctors, too. They did a lot of different tests with me. Dr. Drake said I was a smart little boy. He told Mom I had an IQ in the 140s. All the doctors wanted me to tell them about what was going on at home. At first, I was nervous without Mom there. I told them about the things I wrecked and the voices that told me to do things. Dr. Drake showed me some strange pictures in one of the tests; he asked me to make up stories about them. I told him how I got punished when I was bad, and that I didn't really remember doing most of the things I got in trouble for.

Being at Children's Center wasn't too bad. There were other kids around, and I got to play with them sometimes. Mom and Dad came to visit, but the doctors didn't let Robin, Brian or Doug come. I missed them a lot. I stayed at Children's Center for 10 long days. I thought I'd never get to go home. When Mom and Dad finally came to get me, I was really happy. Everyone treated me well at Children's Center, and I didn't get in any trouble, but I was lonely, especially when I went to bed at night.

Dr. Drake said I was going to come to talk to him every week. So were Mom and Dad.

I didn't know that the doctors wrote everything down, but here is what they wrote in my medical record after my 10 days there.

* * * *

Hospital Course
The child was seen by the Psychologist who felt that the child had above normal intelligence with normal performance (verbal task, visual-motor coordination). He did tasks up to a 6-8 year level. Rorschach's testing revealed thoughts of killing with good repression. The child was also seen by the Psychiatrist; his impression was that Troy was an appealing, active, sturdy 4 11/12-year old boy who related very well and very talkative, with superior intelligence by testing. He was very panicky on admission, but had settled down in the hospital, not being a ward management problem, and heard no voices since being in the hospital by his account. His impression was that the child had acute anxiety manifested by hallucinatory experience and destructive and impulsive

behavior associated with questionable seizure epi-
sodes in history.

Family History
Mother is living and well; she had convulsions at 3
years of age with high fever. The father is living and
well. There are three siblings, 2 boys and 1 girl. The
youngest sibling is 2 years of age.

Diagnosis
Emotional Reaction of Childhood, with Hallucinations

Condition on Discharge
Improved

Prognosis
Presumably good, if Troy continues to respond to the
psychotherapy as he did while he was in the hospital.

Disposition
Troy and his parents will be seen by the Psychiatrist
in Central Psychiatry Clinic.

* * * *

When I came home, Aunt Gloria, Uncle Will and my cousins,
Peggy, Denise, Cheryl and Ray, came to visit us. We always had fun
together. Peggy was older, like my sister. Denise smiled a lot like her
mother. I liked her, and decided I wanted to marry her when we got
older. Ray was kind of small and Cheryl was a baby.

It was a warm, sunny day and Mom had filled our wading pool
with water from the hose. We ran through the pool and splashed
in the cool water. I decided to show off. I grabbed my hula hoop,
and put it over my head, like I was the pole in a ring toss game. I

gave it a hard push and started twirling it around my waist. I twisted and turned, and kept it spinning around my stomach. Everyone was laughing. I was really going fast now, moving my body like I was dancing the Twist. I wanted to keep my hula hoop up forever, but I started to slow down a little as I got tired. I took a few steps backwards and tried to use my legs to keep it up. As the hula hoop dropped down to my thighs, I took another step back. My heels hit the wading pool and I lost my balance. I landed on my back as water splashed high in the air, and then covered my face and body. Pressed against my back at the bottom of the pool, the hula hoop now stood straight up, as if to show its independence.

I wiped the water from my eyes and looked up. Everyone roared uncontrollably with laughter. I looked at Denise, who laughed hard along with everyone else. Now embarrassed, I wished they weren't watching me anymore.

* * * *

Mom was really good at drawing and art. Sometimes she watched the TV show, *You Are An Artist* with host Jon Gnagy, America's first TV art teacher. Mom bought a Gnagy art kit. It had colored pencils and fancy charcoal you could use to fill in your drawing. Mom would sometimes do art projects with us. Robin was good at drawing, just like Mom. Brian and I drew pictures, too, but not like Mom and Robin.

Another project we did that summer was carving figures out of Ivory soap. Mom turned a bar of white Ivory soap into a beautiful, miniature cat. Her carving looked a lot like our real cats, Bandit and Midnight, except for the color. Bandit was orange. Midnight was a shiny, jet black. She was a nice cat; she never scratched anyone.

I liked to watch Mom making her cats. She carved thin slices of soap that looked like vanilla ice cream. Mom let me try, too. I got to use a shiny, gold jackknife. It was a beauty. I tried to do what she did, but my soap looked like a peeled potato cut into bumpy chunks. It was still fun until my knife slipped off the soap one day and sliced into my thumb. The blood turned my carving red. Mom wiped away the blood from my hand and held a damp wash cloth on my thumb to stop the bleeding. The doctor gave me a few stitches. After it healed and I took the bandage off, I had a small scar as a reminder.

I didn't know it, but when I was at Children's Center, Mom told Robin and Brian that I was mentally ill. Mom said that the mentally ill can be very intelligent and tricky.

Even though we talked to Dr. Drake every week, things didn't get better. Mom said I was getting up in the middle of the night and still breaking things and doing other stuff. One morning when I woke up, Mom was there at the foot of my bed.

"Troy, what did you do last night?" she asked.

I could tell something really bad had happened by the way she asked me, and I was in trouble. I had a sick feeling in my stomach.

"I tore the wallpaper in the parlor," I offered.

I could tell right away that was wrong.

"Troy, tell me the truth about what you did," she said with a calm but serious tone.

"I'm not sure," I said. I looked down instead of at her.

"Troy, did you do anything with the food?" she said.

"No, Mom," I said quickly.

I said it with all my heart. I *really* wanted her to believe me.

"Troy, I'll ask you again. Did you do anything to our food?"

"No, Mom."

I began to cry a little. I could feel my heart racing. The bedroom walls felt like they were closing in on me. I couldn't go anywhere and there was nothing I could do or say that would make a difference. She looked really mad. She came at me and turned me over on my stomach, and pinned me on the mattress by leaning on me. Whack, whack, whack. I arched my back and tried to turn my

33

body; it didn't help. I felt the sting and warm rush of blood to the back of my legs. Whack, whack. She shifted her weight and now I couldn't move at all. Whack, whack, whack. Tears streamed down my cheeks and onto my pillow. I stopped trying to get away. It hurt so bad, but there was nothing I could do. I kept hoping she would stop, but she kept on hitting me.

Finally, she let go of me. I wiped my tears and avoided her glance.

"Troy, did you do something to the food for Uncle Sal's dog?"

I thought, no, please, no! I wouldn't try to hurt Uncle Sal's dog. Please, not that.

"No, Mom. I didn't," I pleaded.

"Well, Uncle Sal's dog was poisoned and might die. I want you to tell me the truth this time. Did you poison Uncle Sal's dog?" she said slowly.

"No, Mom .... I .... didn't," I stammered.

She grabbed me and spanked me harder than before. I think the only reason she stopped was that her hands became sore from swatting me. I was worried about Uncle Sal's dog, and I was scared of Mom. I knew I didn't poison his dog. I didn't remember even going near the dog food, and I didn't go near Uncle Sal's dogs because they barked a lot. But I was also worried. .... Maybe I had killed Uncle Sal's dog. How could I do such a terrible thing?

Mom was also worried that I might have poisoned all of our family's food, so she threw it all out. She went shopping again and got all new stuff, even jelly and ketchup and maple syrup.

The summer ended with another big scare. This time, Mom said I had tried to choke Doug. She wasn't in the room when it happened. She asked me a lot of questions. Mom talked to Dr. Drake; he said I should come and stay at Children's Center again.

When we got there, Mom, Dad and I talked to a different psychiatrist. Mom told him that I had stayed at Children's Center before and that we saw Dr. Drake every week. She told him about some of the old things that had happened. He seemed to already know about them, or maybe he just thought that was the type of kid I was. She continued on with the recent things she said I had done.

I thought he'd get angry at me, or at least look mad, but he didn't. He just nodded his head, wrote things down and thought of more questions to ask Mom. This time I stayed for 12 days. It was a lot like the first time. People were nice. I saw Dr. Drake sometimes. All the doctors asked me a lot of questions. I wasn't afraid to answer them. I already knew I wouldn't get in trouble.

I had one test that was sort of weird, but it didn't hurt. They wanted me to fall asleep, but first, they put gray, sticky stuff in my hair. Then they stuck small wires to all the gunk on my head so the wires wouldn't fall off. I must have looked like the inside of a radio or something.

The test was an electroencephalogram, or EEG. They wanted to measure the electrical activity in my brain when I was awake and when I was sleeping. The machine wrote a steady stream of curvy lines on rolls of paper with several pens attached to it. So the test looked at my brain wave patterns, which might show that I had epilepsy. Mom had also told the doctors that when she was three, she had a really high fever and had a seizure. That had horrified Grandma.

"Okay, Troy," said the technician in the room where they were going to do the test. "We want you to lie down on the pillow and stay still. I am going to turn out the lights. You can sleep if you want to. As you rest, the machine will write things down. It won't hurt at all. I'll come and get you when the test is over."

She tucked the blanket in for me and turned the lights out as she left.

I tried hard to keep my head still. I think I fell asleep right away.

It didn't seem like I was sleeping long when she came back in and woke me up.

"Troy. Troy, the test is over," she said in a soft comforting voice.

She helped me sit up, and started gently pulling the wires away from my sticky scalp.

"You did a great job, Troy," she said with enthusiasm.

The next day Mom and Dad came to visit.

"They put some sticky stuff in my hair and then stuck wires to my head. Then they turned out the lights and wanted me to go to sleep," I recounted.

Mom and Dad smiled. Mom said she would make my favorite dinner for me when I came home. I asked her to cook ham and mashed potatoes.

A few days later, Mom and Dad came to pick me up. I was very happy to be going home and back with my family. The medical record told about my second stay at Children's Center in three months, including the results of my EEG.

* * * *

Discharge Summary
This was the second Children's Center admission of this 5 2/12-year-old white male, who was admitted for hallucinations and bizarre behavior in the home.

Present Illness
History reveals that his first admission was for evaluation of the rather sudden onset of auditory hallucinations and questionable visual hallucinations. After discharge, he was followed in the Psychiatric Outpatient Clinic. Recently his behavior has become of great concern to the parents; he apparently attempted to jump from the top of the refrigerator, told his mother that he heard voices on numerous occasions-one

occasion, they told him to go get a knife. He apparently struck his 10 year-old sister's doll's head with a baseball bat, he has threatened members of the family according to the mother, and there is an incident of questionable choking of the youngest brother.

Physical Examination
Temperature was 99.8 degrees, respirations 18, pulse 84, blood pressure 112/70, height 42 inches, weight 45 pounds. This was a sandy-haired, crew-cut, stocky little boy alert and cooperative and intelligent in response to questions and requests. Examination of the head, ears, eyes, nose and throat was within normal limits.

Laboratory Data
Urinalysis was normal. Skull films were normal. An electroencephalogram was normal in both the wake and sleep tracings.

Hospital Course
The patient subsequently underwent psychological testing and was seen by a Psychiatrist. During his hospitalization, his behavior was not considered to be bizarre. He occasionally spoke rather casually of his auditory hallucinations. After a period of observation, it was felt that this child was most likely not psychotic but was suffering from acute emotional reaction to childhood with hallucinations. It was therefore decided to discharge him, and he is to be followed in the Outpatient Clinic and it was hoped that some Nursery School situation could be arranged for this child in order that he may spend some time outside the home.

Diagnosis
Emotional Reaction of Childhood, with Hallucinations
Condition on Discharge
Improved.

Prognosis
Good.

Disposition
To be followed in the Outpatient Clinic with hopes toward Nursery School placement and continued therapy.

* * * *

During the day, Robin and Brian went to Catholic school. I wasn't old enough to go there, but now I was going to attend nursery school. I really looked forward to it. Our teacher was very nice. She read us lots of stories. She gave us big pencils to use and we wrote our names on yellow lined paper. We colored and painted pictures. I liked to draw a house with a chimney and a curving walkway. I drew curly smoke coming out of the chimney and a big red tulip in front of the house. Sometimes I would make it snow by adding a lot of dots in the sky. Mom put one of my pictures on the fridge.

Sometimes at nursery school, we got to play whatever we wanted with the other kids. My favorite was playing with the cardboard bricks. I liked to make tall buildings. We would drive the little cars along the wooden block streets we made between the buildings. Sometimes the cars would crash and the buildings would tumble down, but the teacher didn't get mad at us.

Once a week, Mom, Dad and I went to see Dr. Drake. I talked to him by myself for a little while. So did Mom and Dad. Sometimes we all talked to Dr. Drake together. Mom said that Dr. Drake would help me get better. I liked talking to him and hoped she was right.

But things at home got worse. Dad was still working at night

38

at Cromona's Bakery. Mom was sure that I got up at night and did things, but that I tried to keep it a secret. She stayed up late sometimes to catch me in the act. She even had Robin stay up late with her a few times to watch.

Mom and Dad and Dr. Drake talked about getting me more help. Dr. Drake said I needed inpatient care, and that I should stay somewhere and get more therapy than just seeing him once a week. So in October, Dr. Drake applied to the Evans Development Center to try to get me in there. I didn't know anything about these plans.

In November during one of our weekly visits, Dr. Drake told Mom, Dad and me that he was going to move to Minneapolis because he had a new job there. He said that he liked me and would miss our talks, but I could talk to another psychiatrist so I didn't have to worry. I was going to miss Dr. Drake. I think Mom was going to miss him a lot, too. I didn't know if Dad would.

In December, I had to go to a different place called the Evans Development Center three times to talk to their psychiatrists. The holidays passed. Mom was mad at me a lot. Sometimes she cried even when I didn't do anything. She started tying me in bed at night so I couldn't get up. She'd wrap a sheet around my arms and tie the ends to the sides of the bed. Then she would use another sheet and do the same thing to my legs. I couldn't move much, and she got mad at me if I tried. Sometimes she used her nylon stockings instead of sheets and tied them to my wrists and ankles. The nylons were really tight and hurt. I wet the bed almost every night.

When I woke up in the morning, I had to lie there on my back on my wet sheets until Mom came into the room. Sometimes she let me get up and get washed up. Other times, she asked me a lot of questions about what I had done during the night.

As the situation continued to get worse, here is what Mom wrote in the notes she kept about me.

At times death seems a welcome relief. Yet enough spirit remains in me that I entertain a hope of someday being able to give and enjoy happiness with Russ and the kids as we used to. This situation is so prolonged. Not a minute away from it. And other matters are aggravating, too. Sal and Aunty Rosa give me a pain—yet they have been good to us. Still wish we could live in a single house. Money matters are pressing—washer is breaking down and having to be eternal sentinel prevents my going to launderette. I'm not able to feel safe to nap while Russ watches kids and after Monday night, I'll not go out in a hurry.

Week's rundown

Sun Jan 7 Troy goes after Doug with knife, also tries to choke him. Sunday night, tied in sheet, out of control, raving—crying, screaming, hallucinations.

Mon Jan 8 While I'm at PTA, Russ asleep. Troy up and down from cellar. Russ sends him out of room. Troy gets flying saucer, "coasts" in kitchen. Had baseball bats—hurt, frightened Doug.

Tues Jan 9 Doug very scared—says Troy will kill him when he comes home because Doug didn't kill other kids—says Troy has carving knife. Wild search—finally found in basket in pantry. Russ left it out on pantry counter. Russ not afraid of Troy—thinks Troy would never try to harm him—but might harm us.

Wed Jan 10 Troy not tied since Sunday night. He goes out each night—uses window or front door. When Doug wouldn't let him in living room, he went through snow and shoveled at living room window. Got jackknife from car. Monday night had asked Russ 3-4 times to put it elsewhere.

Thurs Jan 11 Troy scaring Doug, whispering through door, etc. Doug won't eat, says Troy will blow him up with shot gun and says Doug will die and never see me again. Troy tried to strangle Midnight (cat).

Fri Jan 12 Troy in my room with knife, also cut Doug's fingers. In afternoon, went after Doug who hid under bed—pulled Doug out by feet, had knife—we realized he was alone. Robin got there first, Troy heard and went in his room. Took his room apart, can't find knife—black handle knife same as he used on Christmas Day—knife still missing—also jackknife. I beat Troy awful—All of us shook. Kids and me scared.

Sat Jan 13 Here we go—All day today, tonight and 1/2 tomorrow—with no relief in sight. Please God—don't let anything happen to kids—or me either as that would be curtains for kids too.

Mom called Dr. Drake and told him what had been going on with the knives, and that no one in the house was safe. I was now five and a half years old and on my way to Children's Center for the third time. I was scared, and confused. Why was I getting in trouble all the time?

My third stay at Children's Center was similar to the other times.

I had another EEG done; this time the results showed I had a poorly organized, immature pattern for my age. Here is a little more from what the doctor wrote in the Discharge Summary.

* * * *

Chief Complaint
Severe behavior problem, being impossible to handle at home.

Present Illness
This child's previous admissions were because of destructive behavior, visual and auditory hallucinations, and at times he attempted to harm himself and other members of the family. Recently his behavior became intolerable at home, and on several occasions he tried to harm his younger sibling, and expressed ideas of killing his parents or himself. It is of note to mention that he had been attending nursery school, and apparently he was no problem behavior wise while he was among other children and in the school situation. However, all his symptoms and manifestations described in the past appear in the home environment, which make, for the parents, in spite of their decided cooperation and willingness to cope with the problem, an intolerable situation to withstand.

Immediately prior to his admission, the mother found that one of the kitchen knives was missing, and she felt certain that Troy had hidden it and she was unable to find it. Because of the above mentioned factors and symptoms, and in view of the fact that the Psychiatrist in charge of Troy's case is leaving Mason Heights, Troy's case is being currently evaluated at Evans Development Center for treatment in their Inpatient Service. However, in view of the difficult situation at home, Troy is admitted in an acute emergency situation while further arrangements for his admission to the above-named institution are being made.

Hospital Course
Again as before, Troy adjusted very well in the ward environment, was very pleasant and talkative, and did not appear to be preoccupied with any homicidal or suicidal thoughts. After 2-3 days in the hospital, plans were made to have Troy sent to stay with his grandmother, but due to inconvenience of the last hour this could not be done, and he went home instead. He was so angry, disturbed, harmful and unmanageable when he got home that arrangements had to be made for him to be hospitalized on a 10-day temporary care paper.

Condition On Discharge
Unchanged.

Prognosis
Guarded.

* * * *

Dr. Drake arranged for me to go to a state mental institution in Claydale, which is part of Mason Heights. I stayed there for about one week until they could get me into the Central Mental Health Institute in Brantfield.

This was going to be my new home for the next year and a half.

4
Life in a Mental Institution

The MGM movie, Wizard of Oz, was adapted to the big screen in 1939 from the L. Frank Baum children's book, *The Wonderful Wizard of Oz*. Although other versions of the story had been made into movies during the silent film era, Noel Langley, Florence Ryerson, E.A. Wolf and a group of screen writers wrote the script that brought the story to life for generations to come.

As most Americans know, the story revolves around Dorothy, the spunky, teenage farm girl who gets banged in the head and knocked unconscious by a window frame blown in her direction from the fierce winds in a tornado. As she lies dormant in a dream-like state in her bed, Dorothy meets evil and beautiful characters, and follows a sometimes precarious path along the yellow brick road, in an attempt to get back home to her family.

The Wizard of Oz first made its way to prime time TV on November 3, 1956. In a time before cable TV, DVD players and streaming media, the Wizard of Oz aired just once a year. Watching this classic became an annual family ritual, feverishly anticipated by young and old.

* * * *

The last thing that Dr. Drake did before he left for Minneapolis was get me admitted to the Brantfield Mental Health Institute. So on January 21, 1962, I was transferred to Brantfield. It was about a 15-mile drive from Claydale. As we made our way slowly through the traffic, I stared out the window, but didn't notice the bumper to bumper cars or stream of people passing by. The traffic thinned out and we moved along.

We drove into the front entrance of the Brantfield Mental Health Institute, navigating the maze of roads that crisscrossed among the many red brick buildings. Most of the structures were reserved for mentally ill grownups, but with acres of open land and a lot of kids on waiting lists, the state government built and opened Brantfield Children's Unit in 1955. In our family, we just called it Brantfield. It was a place for seriously disturbed, mentally ill kids. No one told me how long I would have to stay, but I hoped it wouldn't be for too long.

They kept the boys on one side of the building and the girls on the other side, separated with a big door at the end of the hallway. They also split us up by age. Brantfield had teenagers up to 16 years old, but they stayed on the fourth floor, which was the top. I was with the youngest boys. At 5 1/2 years old, I might have been the youngest kid there. I know I was one of the smallest.

A man named Mr. Carlson led me down the hallway. He had a lot of keys hanging from his belt and they clacked against his right leg, accenting every other step down the hall. At the end of the corridor was a big blue door that had a narrow, horizontal window that met Mr. Carlson at eye level. It was too high for me to see through, but it had small wire spread through the glass like vines on the side of the building to make it hard for the kids to break. He fumbled through his keys and finally found the right one. He unlocked the door and we went in.

There was a big room on the left with a painting of a large brown tree, the branches sprawling across the wall. There was a colorful bird sitting on the highest limb. Green leaves and blue sky had been sponged across the top. On another wall, a tall window with small rows of glass squares let the remaining minutes of daylight through and made sure that nobody got out.

Like isolated cacti in the open dessert, the boys were spread out in the long room. I immediately noticed a boy standing by himself, crying loudly. At home, the only reason Brian or Doug or I would be crying was if we got into a fight, or Mom was punishing us. The boy's hair was messy and he didn't have any sneakers on. A few kids watched TV, sitting passively on the couch with blank expressions on their faces. Another boy was sitting on the floor and drawing. There were some books with loose bindings and torn pages scattered on the floor.

Mr. Carlson introduced me to everyone, "This is Troy."

Most of the kids kept doing what they were doing and didn't look up.

One of the bigger kids who must have been having a bad day said, "So what."

"Let's be nice, Charlie," said Mr. Carlson.

Mr. Carlson brought me to a room that had a lot of clothes, sheets and blankets piled on shelves.

"Let's grab you a few things to get you started. This is where we keep all the clothes," he said.

He held out a green checkered shirt and measured it against me to see if it fit me. He did the same thing with a pair of striped pants and some pajamas.

"I think you're a small. Ya, definitely a small," he decided.

He grabbed some shirts, socks and underwear. Then he picked up two sheets, a blanket and a pillow case for my bed.

We walked down the hall and into a room with a bed and a small dresser.

"Do you know how to make your bed?" he asked.

46

"Sometimes my mother makes it for me, and I help," I said.

"Well, here's how you do it," he said with a smile.

Then he showed me how to make the bed.

"Okay. It's almost Lights Out time. Change into these pajamas and I'll be back in a few minutes," he said.

I changed quickly and folded my clothes into a neat pile and put them on my bed.

He came back and said, "Good. You changed already. I'll take those clothes from you. You'll get them back when you leave here to go home. Okay, come with me and I'll show you around."

We walked down the hall, with the noisy keys warning some kids that Mr. Carlson was coming, while others didn't notice.

"This is the Rec room. You can play in here on your free time," he said.

There were some toys, some board games, books, a ping pong table and a TV.

"Okay. Thanks," I said with enthusiasm.

"Heh, Mr. Martin. I want you to meet someone. This is Troy. He's from Powell. Mr. Martin works the night shift," he said.

"Glad to have you aboard," he said.

Next we walked down the hall past the other kids' rooms.

"This is where you go if you don't do what you're supposed to do or if you need to cool down. I hope you stay out of here," he said.

It was a room with just a plastic mattress on the floor and no sheets, blankets or pillows. It smelled like someone had just peed on it.

Then a voice seeming to come out of the ceiling said loudly, "Time for lights out. Lights out everyone."

Mr. Carlson chuckled at my startled reaction to the intercom, "Well, it's time for bed. Brush your teeth quickly and get into bed."

I made my way back to my room and got my toothbrush and toothpaste and went into the big bathroom that had sinks, and showers and toilet stalls. It was so much bigger than what we had at home. I brushed my teeth and went to the bathroom one last time. The other kids were doing the same thing. I went back to my room.

"Good night," Mr. Carlson said.

He closed my door, blocking out the light from the hallway. I pulled my pillow tight. I felt all alone. I wondered what everyone was doing at home. Maybe Robin and Brian were watching Lassie or Bugs Bunny on TV. Doug might have been going to bed right then too, with Mom and Dad tucking him in for the night.

I remembered how Mom and Dad would smile while I hummed ta-da, ta-da, ta-da, ta-da and got ready for bed and put everything away really fast. I missed them all so much. I looked around the room. I stared at the crack of light that lined the bottom of the door. I tried, but I couldn't fall asleep. Tears started streaming down my cheeks. I was sure not to make a lot of noise. I didn't want Mr. Carlson or any of the kids to hear me.

In the morning, the door to my room sprung open and another man popped his head in, "You must be Troy. I'm Mr. Stewart. Take your sheets and pillow case off your bed and get ready for breakfast."

I glanced in some of the other rooms as I walked to the bathroom. It didn't take me long to get ready. Some of the kids were taking medicine. Then, we went to the cafeteria. It was a big room with a lot of tables and chairs. I had a bowl of Corn Flakes. The milk came in a little carton.

After that, it was time to go to our school. It was just a short walk to another red brick building, but it was cold. Our teacher met us at the door. I was hoping she was like my nursery school teacher.

"Hi," she said. "You must be Troy."

I nodded my head and barely said ya. She led me to my desk. There were two other kids sitting near me, but they didn't seem to notice me. Mrs. Murphy had long straight hair and a smile on her face that never seemed to go away. There was a big blackboard at the front of the room with writing on it.

She brought me some papers and a pencil and asked me if I knew how to write the alphabet and numbers. I told her I liked doing that. When I was home, sometimes we played school and Robin was the teacher. I liked writing my letters and numbers. Mrs. Murphy showed me what to do and I started writing.

I guess some of the other boys didn't like to do their letters and numbers. They just sat there doing nothing. Sometimes, a kid would start yelling or crying. Mrs. Murphy would ask him to be quiet, but usually that didn't work. When it was time to leave, Mrs. Murphy collected our papers. She seemed happy that I filled up both sides of my paper.

Later in the day, we got to play in the Rec room. I watched cartoons mostly.

I also had to talk to a psychiatrist. He asked me a lot of questions.

"Troy, tell what has been happening with you at home."

I told him that I did a lot of things I wasn't supposed to do, and that Mom punished me when I was bad.

"Well, what things do you do wrong?" he asked.

"Sometimes I get up at night and I wreck things," I answered.

"What do you wreck?" he continued.

"I tear the wallpaper and write on the walls," I said sheepishly.

"Why do you do that?"

"I am jealous of my brothers. Mom asks me about all the things I do, but I don't remember doing them," I said.

I told him that Mom spanked me when I was bad. He asked me about the voices that I heard and I told him what I told the other doctors, that they told me to do things.

"Have you heard any voices today?"

"No," I said.

Psychiatrists always seemed to ask the same questions. Was I mad at Mom, or Dad? How did I get along with Robin and my brothers? After we talked for awhile, he told me he would see me again soon. When I got back to the Rec Room, that big kid Charlie was yelling and crying. I couldn't tell what was wrong, but it took two of the counselors to pick him up and take him out of the Rec room. I wondered if Charlie had to go to that room with the smelly mattress on the floor.

When it was time to go to bed, I thought about all my stuffed animals that I lined up on my pillow on my bed at home, with their feet tucked under the covers. There was barely enough room for me to slide into bed without squishing them. There was plenty of room in my new bed. I missed them, but I tried real hard not to cry.

The next day was a lot like the one before it. At Brantfield, we followed a schedule for everything. We got up and made our beds and got changed. A lot of kids took their medicine. We ate breakfast and then lined up for school. Sometimes we got to play games in the gym. I liked doing that. I learned how to do a fancy soccer kick, sliding my right foot behind the heel on my left foot and kicking the ball. Some of the older kids were good playing ball, but some just stood there not doing anything.

On good nights, we got to watch a movie and have a snack before bed. I got to see an Elvis Presley movie. I think he was in the Army or something like that because he had to wear a uniform. He got into a couple of fights and beat up the bad guys. He sang a lot of songs, too. I liked him.

Mom, Dad, Robin, Brian and Doug came on Visiting Day. I was so excited to see them all. Since it was cold outside, all the families had to stay in the gym. Mom brought a blanket and a picnic lunch, with all kinds of good things to eat.

Mom spread out the blanket on the hard gym floor, and we sat on it, looking like we were staying afloat on our own small iceberg in the Arctic. I felt a little awkward with my family. I didn't know what to say. Maybe we all felt like that because we were quiet at first. Then Mom broke the silence, "So do you like the food here, Troy?"

"Ya. I like breakfast the best," I answered.

"What do they have?" she asked.

"We have cereal and toast, and sometimes eggs. They have these little milks," I said, and measured out how small the carton was with my hands.

"Are the kids nice?" Dad asked.

"Ya. They seem nice."

"Are any of these kids on your floor?" Mom asked.

I pointed out a few kids, but some of them didn't have any visitors.

Robin and Brian seemed to be looking around the gym at the smattering of other Brantfield kids with their families. You could tell which ones were the Brantfield kids by the mismatched, wrinkled clothes. That's what I had on, too, but I tucked my shirt in. A few Brantfield kids didn't have any shoes on. Either they forgot to put them on, or maybe the counselors took them away, because they tried to run away. A lot of these kids were different from the kids at home, staring off into space or swaying back and forth.

"Where do you sleep at night?" asked Robin.

"I sleep in a room by myself. They say 'Lights out' on a loud speaker and we all have to go to bed. They close the door and turn off all the lights. It gets pretty dark."

I told them about our school and the Rec room.

I asked Mom when I would be able to come home, but she didn't know. She said the psychiatrists would try to help me. I told her that I had talked to a psychiatrist a few times already.

"What is his name, Troy?" she asked.

"I don't know, but maybe he is helping me already," I said.

Mom brought a deck of cards and we played crazy eight. Brian had a small kick ball that we tried. I showed everyone the new soccer kick I learned, but it was crowded in the gym so we couldn't kick the ball around. The time went by fast, and then it was time for my family to leave. Everyone hopped off the blanket, our portable family home, and Dad folded it up.

I really wanted them to stay longer. No, I really wanted to leave with them. I thought about how I used to hide down low in the back seat of our car when Dad had to go back to work. I wanted Mom and Dad to say that everything was better, and take me home with them right then. But that did not happen. As we said goodbye, I felt like a loser in tug of war. Brantfield was pulling me back to my ward. For two hours, it felt like my family was taking me back. But they couldn't hold on to the rope any longer. Mom, Dad, Robin, Brian and Doug were going home. Brantfield won.

We hugged each other and I tried not to cry. I hurt inside. I wanted to be with my family so much. Why couldn't I go home with them? Just like when I was at Children's Center, I didn't get in any trouble here. I knew I could be good at home if they just gave me another chance.

With Dr. Drake in Minneapolis, Dr. Culver was now my psychiatrist at Brantfield. I saw him a few times when I first got there, and then once a week after that. He was easy to talk to and he saw how I acted on my ward and in school.

Nobody told me, but Dr. Culver totally disagreed with Dr. Drake's diagnosis of me. Dr. Drake felt that I needed two or three years of intensive psychiatric therapy, and that I couldn't stay at home until I went through this treatment. Mom wrote in her notebook that he suggested I might have to live in a foster home for awhile instead of coming right back home. It was possible that I might never be able to live at home again.

That's not what Dr. Culver thought. He told Mom and Dad that his diagnosis was that I was not mentally or emotionally ill, but that I suffered from an unhappy home life and was not given enough love. He said that I probably would be better off in a foster home if my home life did not change. After relying on Dr. Drake to arrange three hospitalizations at Children's Center psychiatric ward, meeting with Mom and Dad to work on their problems, and committing me to a mental institution in Brantfield to get inpatient care, Mom and Dad must have felt like they got slapped in the face when they heard what Dr. Culver had to say.

Mom was furious. She was not going to stand by and let this doctor misdiagnose my problem and prevent me from getting proper treatment. She got in touch with Mr. Cummings, a psychiatric social worker at Brantfield and told him about all of my problems, what Dr. Drake had said about me, the long waiting lists to get me into any inpatient facility, and finally Dr. Drake being able to get me into Brantfield. Now, Dr. Culver was jeopardizing my care. Given all that had happened, how could he think that I was fine? If Dr. Culver was not going to give me the care I needed, then Mom said she would find another psychiatrist outside of Brantfield to evaluate me. Mom said that Mr. Cummings told her that they didn't allow this type of consultation.

Everything was falling apart. So Mom called Dr. Drake in Minneapolis to let him know what was going on. Dr. Drake suggested that Mom call Dr. Plummer, a colleague from Children's Center, and explain the situation. Dr. Drake said that I had the ability to fool people into thinking that I was not ill, and, for that reason, sometimes it might be difficult to get me appropriate care.

Mom also called Dr. McGill, the Obstetrician who helped deliver all of us kids and someone Mom considered a friend. Dr. McGill agreed with Mom and couldn't understand how Dr. Culver came up with his diagnosis.

Mom called Dr. Plummer at Children's Center and told him that

Dr. Drake, now in Minneapolis, suggested she give him a call. She rehashed the history of my problems, and what Dr. Culver from Brantfield had said. Dr. Plummer called Dr. Jarrett, the head of the Children's Unit at Brantfield, to get to the bottom of the situation.

Then Dr. Plummer called Mom to let her know how the discussion went. Dr. Jarrett had said that they did not feel that I was as sick as the other kids at Brantfield. He suggested it would be better for me if I either went to a different institution for kids that had less severe problems, or that I got placed in a foster home. Dr. Jarrett assured that the Department of Mental Health would remain involved and make sure that I received follow-up care. Dr. Plummer recommended to Mom that she go along with Dr. Jarrett's recommendation.

So Mom began to look into alternatives to Brantfield. She talked to Monsignor Reddington, a director of the Catholic Charitable Bureau. Despite showing interest and compassion about my situation, he was not able to give support as the Catholic diocese did not have any facilities that could help me. The Catholic institutions, St. Bernadette's and Blake, were for retarded or disabled children.

In a letter to Dr. Drake in Minneapolis, Mom said that she felt encouraged by Dr. Plummer from Children's Center, but that she had little faith in Brantfield. She said she had heard different messages from Brantfield depending on whether she was talking to Dr. Jarrett, Dr. Culver or Mr. Cummings, the social worker. She said they had told her different things at different times. One was that I would be put in a group placement, and continue to receive psychological treatment. Later they said I would be placed in a foster home through the Department of Public Welfare, and that I would no longer be followed by the Department of Mental Health or receive any psychological treatment. And then, finally, that I would remain at Brantfield indefinitely.

And then Mom said, there was Dr. Barrett, the head of the entire facility at Brantfield. Since I had such a high IQ, Dr. Barrett was personally interested in my case and would see to it that I got the specialized schooling that I needed.

Mom also said that Dr. Plummer from Children's Center had told her not to accept Mr. Cummings' claim that consultations from doctors outside of Brantfield would not be allowed. n fact, Dr. Plummer said he had personally consulted on several cases at Brantfield.

Mom left no stone unturned. She had kept Grampa, her father who worked for the federal government up to date on the problems with my care. Grampa spoke to a child psychiatrist who was coming to Mason Heights to see someone at the McCauley Clinic for adolescent children, one of the places that Mom had called when I was first having problems. At Grampa's request, this child psychiatrist contacted Dr. Plummer about me. When the psychiatrist next spoke to Grampa, he said to have Mom insist on getting an outside psychiatrist involved. He suggested three psychiatrists to Grampa, and said that any of them would be good.

By this point, Dr. Plummer called Mom to tell her about his conversation with the child psychiatrist. One of the three psychiatrists suggested to Grampa was Dr. Gedding from McCauley Clinic. Dr. Plummer recommended that Mom give Dr. Gedding a call and ask him to consult on my case. He felt that Dr. Gedding would be an excellent choice, and, in fact, had already spoken to him about me.

In the meantime, I was getting used to being at Brantfield. Charlie continued to get himself in trouble. One minute he would be sitting calmly watching TV, but then he would try to change the channel or take a toy from another kid, and suddenly he would be yelling and screaming and swinging at anyone in reach. There was another boy I felt bad for. He mostly sat by himself. He didn't like it when other kids were near him. Sometimes he just sat there and cried. A few times at Lights Out, he cried really loud. It made me feel sad, too.

I got along with the kids okay I guess, but I didn't have any good friends that I played with. It was sort of like we were all together in one room, but usually not doing things together. The counselors would get mad at some of the kids when they caused trouble or wouldn't do what they were supposed to do, but they were nice to me. I always did what they told me to do.

School was pretty good, as long as the other kids weren't yelling or crying. Mrs. Murphy liked the pictures I drew, especially the flowers.

One of my favorite things was playing Bombardment in the gym. The counselors stood at the ends of the room and would throw big kick balls at all of us. You had to try to not to get hit with the ball. If you got hit, you had to sit on the side until the game was over. Then everyone would get back in the middle and we would play again. Some of the kids would lie and say that the ball didn't touch them even when it clearly did. I was good at turning my body sideways and jumping up just in time to keep from getting bonked. Sometimes, I was the last kid left in the middle.

We also did tumbling on mats. Mr. Carlson showed me a neat way to do a flip. He lay on his back on the mat with his feet flat on the floor and his knees bent. I ran towards him and put my hands on his knees and pushed off with my feet, doing almost a hand stand. As I started to fall forward, Mr. Carlson put his hands on my shoulders and pushed me through the air right over him. I landed on my feet on the mat. Most of the other kids couldn't figure out how to do it, or were afraid they would get hurt. I couldn't wait to tell Mom and Dad about it.

The days started to get a little warmer, and sometimes we got to go outside. They had a big playground in the back of our building. There were swings, a slide and a big thing that you could push and make go really fast, and then jump on it as it spun around and around. Charlie was really good at pushing it, but sometimes it would go too fast and make me dizzy. One of my favorite things in the playground was the monkey bars. They had two kinds of them. One was shaped like an upside down U. I climbed it like a ladder, working my up to the highest point in the middle and then making my way down the other side, feet first. The other set of monkey bars was harder for me to climb, but I liked it better. I climbed the ladder to the top, and then tried to grab the horizontal bars that looked like rungs of a ladder to swing back and forth. When I got going, I would let go and reach with my right hand to grab the next rung. It felt like my left arm stretched like an elastic and my fingers would start to slip. Sometimes, I wouldn't make it and I'd fall to the ground. But I was getting better at it, and I could usually rock back and forth and grab a few rungs before I landed on the grass below.

It was too cold to think about swimming yet, but there was a pool that the older kids said we could go in when it got hot in the summer. It sounded like fun, but I wanted to be home by the summer and go in Lake Cramby.

Mom, Dad, Robin, Brian and Doug came to visit me every week. When it was warm enough, we all went outside. I liked that a lot better than sitting around in the crowded gym. It didn't matter if other kids were there, when we were outside we could run around and play together just like we were home. I thought a lot about Visiting Day on Sunday and seeing my family. But Visiting Day also made me sad because I knew I had to stay and my family was going to leave. Then I had to patiently wait for the next Visiting Day for them to come back.

I had a lot of time to think about stuff. One of the good things was that I didn't get in any trouble at Brantfield. The counselors never said I got up at night and wrecked things. They never asked me a bunch of questions about what I had done. They never hit me.

Following Mom's phone calls and letter to Dr. Drake, he wrote back to Mom on March 24, 1962.

* * * *

Dear Mrs. Kane,

Many thanks for your lengthy letter bringing me up to date on what has happened with Troy, the family and you since you phoned me.

I can only fully support your continued and concerted efforts to work things out for all of you and get the help you need. I certainly feel you are facing the issues involved as clearly as is possible while at the same time being caught in the middle of what at times must seem like a nightmare. I am fully in accord with your feelings that Troy cannot be home with you now or in the near future, at the same time appreciating your feelings of wanting to hold on to him, and of being depressed and guilty.

I am also in accord with you getting an additional consultation from Dr. Gedding, who is a friend of mine and an excellent psychiatrist. I will write him to make use of Troy's records at Children's Center, which has copies of the summary letters I sent to the Evans Development Center and to Brantfield Mental Health Institute, as well as a record of Troy's treatment. I will also take the liberty of sending him a photostat of your letter to me to bring him up to date on the situation.

I am also very glad that you have gotten connected with the Evans Development Center to continue getting help yourself now when you need it most.

58

Please continue to keep me informed of what is developing as is useful and necessary to you. Thank you for your warm feelings towards me.

Best regards to Troy, Russ, the family and you.

Sincerely,

Matthew Drake, MD

* * * *

Mom and Dad met with Mr. Cummings at Brantfield. He brought up the idea of possibly transferring me to the Crystal Home for Children in Parker. The Crystal Home was the first neuropsychiatric hospital in the country for children. It was named for a girl who came down with encephalitis when she was seven years old. As a result of her disease, she ended up with epilepsy, mental retardation and cerebral palsy. Her parents searched worldwide for a cure for their suddenly-afflicted daughter. At the time, there weren't a lot of hospitals able to deal with such issues, and the few that existed, were for adults. The parents were not able to change the course of their daughter's disabilities, but upon their own deaths, they left their estate as payment and requested that a treatment facility be built for children. So in 1931, the Crystal Home opened its doors to treat children.

Mr. Cummings said that The Crystal Home was an excellent place for children with mental and emotional problems. Mom and Dad wanted to look into The Crystal Home a little more, but said that if it was as good as he said, they would sign the application to try to move me there.

Mom called Dr. Gedding. He said that he would be happy to consult, and asked that Mom make arrangements with Brantfield for him to visit me.

When Mom called Mr. Cummings to ask to arrange the consultation by Dr. Gedding, Mr. Cummings said that Dr. Culver felt his assessment of me was accurate and they would not approve Dr. Gedding's consult. Mom asked Mr. Cummings if they needed my parents' signatures before they could move me out of Brantfield, and he confirmed that they did need their signatures. Mom quickly countered that she would not sign anything until she was able to have another doctor evaluate me. Brantfield approved the consultation by Dr. Gedding, who concurred with Dr. Drake's assessment of me.

Mom's return letter to Dr. Drake spelled out the struggles to arrange the consult and the difficulties with Brantfield and Mr. Cummings. At the end of the two-page letter, she turned her focus to me.

* * * *

Of Troy, himself, he is receiving no treatment (verified by Mr. Cummings). He is seemingly indifferent when we see him each Sunday. He never mentions the other children. He does say each time that he likes living at Brantfield best and that he'd never want to be home again. At times he has seemed not as bright to me and other times he seems more like himself. He seems to be shutting himself off from us. He volunteers very little conversation, ignores our questions at times and seems anxious for us to leave long before time is up.

* * * *

The counselors told us that the Wizard of Oz was going to be on TV, and we were going to be able to watch it that night. I had seen it the year before and really liked it. All the kids were excited.

"Get in a straight line. And everyone has to be quiet or you are not going to see the movie," said one of our counselors.

I stood as straight and tall as I could. I clamped my lips shut, and could hear my breath going in and out of my nose.

"I mean it. Quiet down or you will go back to your rooms," Mr. Martin warned.

I was getting worried that Charlie was going to start yelling and wreck it for everyone. We walked to the dining room. There were a lot of kids. They had wheeled in a TV. I got a good seat, fairly close to the TV. There were people in the kitchen making peanut butter and jelly sandwiches for a snack. The peanut butter was different at Brantfield than at home. It was thicker and dry, and I could smell it. The counselors gave each of us two triangles of white bread, filled with peanut butter and jelly. Maybe it was because I was hungry or excited that night, but that snack with orange juice tasted better than any other I had had there.

They turned down the lights and all the kids clapped. Then the movie started. There was Dorothy on the farm. She had ponytails like Robin had sometimes. Dorothy fell off the fence into the mud next to the pigs. Zeke jumped over the fence and saved her. Dorothy's Aunty Em came out and yelled at them, but she gave them some donuts too. The donuts made me think of Dad.

Dorothy visited Professor Marvel, and Dorothy's dog, Toto, ate one of his hot dogs. All the kids laughed. Then a tornado came, and Dorothy got smacked on the head by a window and knocked out. Suddenly, her house was flying in the air. She looked out the window and two guys in a canoe paddled their way through the air. We all laughed. Dorothy met the cute Munchkins. They sang and danced for her. All of us were afraid of the Evil Witch of the West, who wanted to get Dorothy.

Dorothy liked the munchkins and the good witch, but she wanted to go home. The good witch told Dorothy to go see the Wizard of Oz. He would help her. Dorothy followed the yellow brick road and made some new friends, the Scarecrow, Cowardly Lion and Tin Man. They helped her get to the Land of Oz. Everyone said the Wizard of Oz would help her get home, and give the Scarecrow a brain, the Cowardly Lion some courage, and the Tin Man a heart.

They had to walk down a long, scary hallway before they could ask the Wizard for help. The Lion stopped a few times. He said he was too scared to ask the Wizard for some courage. But Dorothy said they would ask the Wizard for him.

There was fire and smoke as they got to the end of the hallway. Then the Wizard of Oz's head was floating in the air right on top of the fire and smoke. "I am Oz, the great and powerful!" he bellowed.

The Scarecrow, Cowardly Lion, Dorothy and the Tin Man locked arms and tried to stop shaking because they were so scared. Dorothy tried to ask the Wizard if he would help, but he yelled at her. Then he yelled at the Tin Man and Scarecrow. The Wizard of Oz seemed mean. When the Wizard yelled at the Cowardly Lion, the lion fainted. Dorothy got mad, and yelled right back at the Wizard. She said they only came to ask him for some help. Then the Wizard seemed nicer and said he would help them all, if they got the witch's broom from her and brought it back.

The Wizard told them to go. They hesitated for a second and the Wizard screamed, "Go" in a deep voice. The lion got really scared, and ran as fast as he could and dove head first through a window at the end of the hallway. My heart pounded. Just then, one of the counselors turned on the lights and turned off the TV.

"Okay. Time for bed. Everyone get in line," he said.

All the kids groaned. Weren't we going to get to see the rest of the movie? The answer was no. We had to go back to our rooms and go to bed.

I couldn't believe they didn't let us watch the whole movie. I wondered if Robin, Brian and Doug were watching it.

5
Epilepsy, Seizures and Secrets

The history of epilepsy dates back thousands of years. In that time span, epilepsy has been known as the falling disease because of the violent convulsions and lack of body control that some people experience, and the sacred disease by others who believed that spirits invaded the bodies of those afflicted with it. Hippocrates, who lived four centuries before Christ was born, is credited with being one of the first people to attribute epilepsy to physical problems with the brain.

While epilepsy is often associated with severe seizure activity, there are many forms of the disease that reveal itself in much more subtle ways, which can make it difficult to diagnose. Epilepsy occurs most often in children and older adults.

* * * *

Mom continued to read about psychology and medicine. She was convinced that I had some form of epilepsy. Not the kind where my body jerked around uncontrollably and I lost consciousness. Everyone would have seen that. Instead, she thought I had a form of the disease that made me sometimes fade out and not pay attention. She had told the doctors that I did that sometimes. She also had been saying for some time that I complained about the smell of my food, which could also be a symptom. While she thought that maybe I had less noticeable seizures, she still believed that I had them.

If that was true, other people may have seen me having one of these seizures, especially the people who were around me a lot. She thought they must have seen it.

Mom went to Robin and Brian first. She sat them down in the living room and closed the curtains, a sign she wasn't fooling around. She asked them about seeing me having a seizure. She explained that it might be something like my arm twitching or my eyes blinking or my body stiffening up. She said maybe at the time they didn't realize what it was, but if they thought about it, they probably had witnessed it.

Robin and Brian didn't remember me doing these things. Mom told them to think about it a little more. They might be able to remember something if they thought about the times they were with me. Again, Robin and Brian said no.

But Mom persisted. She asked them a lot of questions. Similar to a courtroom lawyer, she hopped on their answers to form the next line of questions. They kept saying no, they hadn't seen me shaking or trembling or blinking or twitching. As the interrogation intensified, Mom's anger became more visible, which exerted more pressure on them. Finally, Brian was either tricked or he gave in. He agreed that maybe he had seen me doing something like she was describing.

Mom let Brian go in the other room, but she continued on with Robin. Hadn't I had a seizure? Hadn't Robin seen it? Mom pressed on until Robin finally tripped up over one of her questions, and said the wrong thing by accident. Robin tried to explain that she hadn't meant to say what she had said, but Mom would not hear of it. Robin had admitted to what Mom suspected.

As a young child, Mom had had a seizure caused by a very high fever. Grandma had reacted like some demon had temporarily overtaken her daughter. Next, Mom looked for proof that Grandma knew about my seizures. Mom reasoned that Grandma babysat us a lot, and must have seen me having a seizure, although she did not apply the same logic to herself or Dad. Mom was intense and determined. She asked Robin if she knew if Grandma had seen me have a seizure. Wasn't it true that Grandma had given Robin a manicure so she wouldn't tell Mom about my seizures? Robin held out as long as she could, but finally she gave in and went along with what Mom had been suggesting: Grandma knew about my seizures.

Mom had her proof.

Like turbulent water going over a waterfall, Mom's energy and anger were surging. She and Dad went to see Grandma. Mom accused Grandma of knowing that I had seizure problems and was keeping them a secret. Grandma denied the whole thing as the argument escalated. Mom also talked to Uncle Hank and told him all about what Grandma had supposedly done. Uncle Hank and Mom also argued. When the dust settled from the accusations and intense arguments, Mom said that Grandma was out of our lives completely. She could no longer babysit for us or see us at all. Uncle Hank and his family, and other relatives on that side of the family, also no longer existed as far as Mom was concerned.

When she went home, Mom used a pair of scissors to cut Grandma out of all the family photographs. That day Robin, Brian and Doug lost a grandmother. Being in Brantfield, I didn't know anything about their big fight or that I wouldn't see Grandma or Uncle Hank and his family again for years. Robin was devastated. She loved Grandma and felt like it was her fault for Grandma being banished from our world.

Mom continued her correspondence with Dr. Drake, letting him know what was going on with me and her own challenges. Dr. Drake's return letter, dated May 11, 1962, showed his continuing support.

* * * *

Dear Mrs. Kane,

Thanks very much for your very long letter.

I can well understand how overwhelming it has been for you to find out all the things Troy has done, especially the whole episode the night of the PTA meeting. Also, the many feelings about your mother which are coming up are likewise upsetting, though certainly very much connected with your feeling depressed and helpless now as you did in the past. I am glad you are on the waiting list at the Evans Development Center, and hope Russ and you get started in treatment soon.

I am glad to hear Troy is still in Brantfield, and that they are looking into his going to the Crystal Home for Children. This would be a good place for him.

Feel free to write me again as would be helpful to you. My best regards to Russ, the children and you.

Sincerely,

Matthew Drake, MD

* * * *

As the days got longer and warmer, we were able to go outside a lot more at Brantfield. Sometimes the counselors would take us for a walk in the nearby woods. And I really loved the playground. I

66

taught myself how to wrap my legs through the monkey bars, bending my legs and resting the back of my knees on the bar. Then I would lower myself and swing back and forth while hanging upside down.

They also had bikes. One day, Mr. Carlson said to me, "Do you want to learn how to ride a bike?"

I had my red push-pedal car at home, but I hadn't been old enough for my own bike.

"Sure," I said, eyeing the blue bike.

"Well, come give it a try," he said.

He helped me get up on the seat. My feet barely reached the pedals.

"I'm big enough to ride it!" I shouted.

Mr. Carlson guided me along as I began to pump my legs, around and around. We were going along pretty good when I realized that Mr. Carlson wasn't holding on anymore.

"You're doing it yourself," he said.

I looked back and Mr. Carlson was jogging just behind me and the bike. The wheels started to wobble, and Mr. Carlson grabbed the back seat and handle bars.

"I can ride a bike!" I exclaimed.

With more practice, I learned how to ride the bike by myself. I couldn't wait to show my family when they came to visit.

One day, Mr. Carlson asked me if I wanted to go home with him on the weekend and meet his family. I felt a little nervous about it, but I liked him so I said okay. The next few days, I wondered what it would be like going to Mr. Carlson's house.

On Friday, we walked out to the parking lot and hopped in Mr. Carlson's red Volkswagen Beetle and flicked on the radio.

"Troy, I think you are going to have fun. You'll like my wife and my daughter, Kristen. She's about your age," he said.

As he drove away from Brantfield, I glanced at Mr. Carlson. His hair was blonde and he had long sideburns. He looked a little younger than Dad. An Elvis Presley song was playing on the radio. I had seen Elvis in a movie on TV, with him singing and beating up the bad guys.

Mr. Carlson tapped his hands on the steering wheel, keeping beat with the music. When we stopped at a red light, he played the drums on his dashboard.

We pulled into Mr. Carlson's driveway in front of his small trailer home. Not knowing what to expect, I now wondered if I should have stayed in Brantfield. Mrs. Carlson met us at the door. She had a warm, friendly smile.

"You must be Troy. Dave always says what a nice boy you are," she said.

I didn't know Mr. Carlson's first name. I had never even thought about him having a first name.

"And this is Kristen," said Mr. Carlson.

I looked down and meekly said hi. Kristen was wearing bright yellow shoes made out of wood.

"Kristen, why don't you get Troy a pair of clogs he can wear?" Mr. Carlson asked.

"These clogs come from Holland, where Dave's family is from. The farmers in Holland used to wear them to keep their feet dry in the fields," Mrs. Carlson explained.

Kristen brought me in my own pair of clogs to wear. I slipped my feet into them. As I did laps around their braided rug, my feet banged up against the inside of the clogs like a bumper car hits the surrounding protective wall. We watched TV and played a few of Kristen's games. For supper, Mr. Carlson cooked hamburgs on a charcoal grill just like Dad did sometimes. Kristen and I played on the swings in the back yard while Mr. Carlson cooked.

At nighttime, they set up a cot for me to sleep on. Mr. Carlson and Mrs. Carlson came in to say good night. Mrs. Carlson tucked me in. I knew they weren't my family, but it still felt good.

Kristen let me try her bike the next day. After lunch, it was time to say goodbye and go back to Brantfield. Mrs. Carlson patted me on the head.

"I hope you can come visit us again. We loved having you here," she said.

I got back in the car, and Mrs. Carlson and Kristen waved good-bye as we pulled out of the driveway and made our way back to Brantfield.

* * * *

After the fallout with Grandma and Uncle Hank, Mom wanted to move away from Powell. She and Dad started to think about buying a house. Grampa offered to help them with the down payment.

Mom and Dad looked at houses and finally found one in Southgate, about 15 miles and three towns south of Powell. Mom was very excited telling me about it on Visiting Day There was a lot more room and we even would have our own back yard.

Mom continued to talk to the doctors and Mr. Cummings at Brantfield about trying to get me better care at a different institution. I didn't know anything about this. Brantfielc was okay, but I wanted to be home. Mom continued to keep Dr. Drake informed about what was going on. This was his response to her latest letter.

* * * *

July 30, 1962

Dear Mrs. Kane,

Thanks for your most recent letter.

I am glad you are feeling more hopeful about yourself as well as Troy. The prospect of moving to a home in Southgate must also be something to

69

look forward to.

As you say in your letter, it is hard for me to respond except in a general way to the questions you asked. In general, I would encourage you to be guided by the hospital recommendations about Troy. I would doubt that his being home for more than weekend visits or comparable short visits is indicated until he has a longer period of hospital treatment. If it is desirable for him to be transferred for further treatment to the Crystal Home for Children, and this can be arranged, I would encourage you to go along with it even though he would be farther away from you. As you know, the goal of his hospital treatment is to help him handle his feelings more satisfac- torily so that he is going to get along at home without being so disturbed. Your own treatment and Russ' at the Evans Development Center will certainly help you when you're able to get started.

As for the questions of your mother and some of the things Brian and Robin have said she has done (as well as Troy), there is obviously no way of knowing for certain how much is fact and how much fantasy. Certainly some has been fantasy and Brian and Robin have been upset by the feelings they've had. Undoubtedly, what is most important for you is getting your own feelings about your mother worked out in therapy.

I am sorry I can't suggest anything further.

I continue to feel that you have shown great courage and a capacity to go on living your life under very trying conditions. I am glad you have managed to get the help you need, and can only hope that in time you will get your own feelings worked out more satisfactorily. I share similar feelings for Troy and Russ.

Again, thanks for your letter. Please continue to feel free to write me as it is useful for you.

My best regards to Russ, Troy, the family and you.

Sincerely,

Matthew Drake, MD

* * * *

In the meantime, Mom and Dad had told Uncle Sal and Aunty Rosa about the house in Southgate, and that they were moving out. So Uncle Sal and Aunty Rosa advertised the upcoming vacancy and started to the show the apartment to potential tenants. It didn't take long before they found a new family to occupy the first floor on 10 Omni Street. However, a few weeks before the sale went through on the new house, the people in Southgate backed out of the deal. They decided not to sell their house. Although he hadn't said so before, Dad now brought up that he was glad because he had never wanted to live in Southgate, but would have gone along with it.

Mom had talked to Mr. Cummings a number of times about her unhappiness with my treatment at Brantfield, but she never felt there were any changes. So Mom called Mr. Cummings and asked about me going to the Crystal Home, which had sounded like such a good fit months before. Mr. Cummings informed Mom that the application had never been submitted. She was furious.

Even though the house in Southgate fell through, Mom and Dad still had to move out of their apartment, because Uncle Sal had rented it out. Mom and Dad did not have enough time to find another house right away, so they decided to get an apartment and look for another house to buy. They found an apartment in Belport, a small coastal town just north of Mason Heights. On one side of Belport was the skyline and the setting sun. On the other side was a large sea wall stretching the length of the beach, separating the open harbor from the neighborhood houses that were packed closely together.

The apartment, halfway up Ocean View Ave., was only a few hundred yards from the beach. Robin and Brian missed the first few weeks of school while the move was being arranged. Since Grandma was not part of our family anymore and we didn't know anyone in Belport, Robin became the family's babysitter for Brian and Doug whenever Mom and Dad were not there.

In September, I started first grade in Brantfield. I liked my teacher and school, but I hadn't been home for eight months. All the talk about a new apartment, right next to the beach, made it even tougher to be away. Part of me loved to hear about walking on the beach and the crabs and fish and pieces of driftwood, broken off from boats or lobster traps. I tried to picture it. I wanted to see where my family lived. I wanted to come home.

I'm not sure if Mom pushed for it or the doctors at Brantfield suggested it would be a good idea, but I was finally able to go home for a few weekends in the fall. The beach was as good as everyone had said, even better. It was the fall so we couldn't go swimming, but that didn't matter because the beach was like an enormous playground.

At the top of our street, there was a thick ocean wall that held the blue-green water back during high tide and big storms. We took walks along the beach. Parts of the shore had rocks all along it. For me, they were like practice baseballs waiting to be tossed into the inviting ocean. Sometimes we heaved big rocks off the jetty into the water below, waiting for the splash and kerplunk. At low tide, we could see the starfish and barnacles stuck to the big rocks, which were lined with green seaweed that looked like grass. The waves slowly built and then crashed against the shore and sea wall with sand and rocks scattering. As the next wave got ready to break, the undertow dragged anything on the shoreline back into the ocean. I was mesmerized by the waves, which never got tired.

At low tide, we walked along the moist, tan-colored sand. The water acted like a big eraser, smoothing away the day's activity and leaving behind a totally new canvas. I drew pictures and wrote my name in the sand with a piece of driftwood that served as my temporary pencil.

But when I wasn't running and playing on the beach and was in our new apartment, it felt sort of strange. I had been away for three-quarters of a year. Doug was three years old now. My family was nice to me, but I felt like an outsider. I was. As the weekend went on, things became more natural.

In the afternoon, my whole family took a walk along the beach. Robin's friend, Betty, also came along. We ended up standing next to the big wall on Atlantic Boulevard. There were some teenagers hanging around not too far from us, fooling around and being kind of noisy. The cars flowed along Atlantic Boulevard like the ebb and flow of the ocean. A blue station wagon packed with a large family drove by heading north, maybe on their way to the amusement park rides at nearby Stockford Beach. A man on his way home came from the other direction and turned right onto Summer Ave.

We leaned against the wall, and took it all in. Dad said that later we could take a ride and get an ice cream cone. Mom told me the story again of how she had craved coffee ice cream when she was pregnant with me. Dad used to buy it for her at the grocery store at the top of Omni Street. She said I must have been able to taste it in her belly, because that was now my favorite kind.

A car filled with teenagers came speeding by. One of the kids was hanging out the window and yelling at the teenagers near us. Suddenly he threw something out of the car window. It was lit, but it wasn't a cigarette. It bounced on the sidewalk right in front of us and hit Mom in the leg. Boom! It exploded. We all ducked. Mom reached down and grabbed her leg. I felt a sharp pain in my ear lobe. Mom's leg was bleeding and she was in pain.

At first, I wasn't sure what had happened. The teenagers by the wall looked over at us, but didn't come to help. It must have been some sort of prank; the kids had thrown a small homemade bomb and hit Mom. She needed to have a doctor look at it. Belport had a small hospital, but Mom and Dad didn't really know where it was. Robin's friend, Betty, said she could show us how to get there. So we all got into our car and Dad drove there.

The doctors cleaned out the cut. The teenagers must have made the bomb themselves, because there was wood and paper and other stuff in Mom's open wound. My ear lobe wasn't cut, but a piece of the bomb was embedded in it, a souvenir I would have for several years. While waiting for the doctors to take care of Mom's leg, Betty asked Robin why I only was home sometimes on weekends. Robin told her that I was extremely intelligent and I went to a special boarding school for gifted children.

I was upset to see Mom get hurt. I made sure I was good and didn't get in any trouble with Mom all weekend. As the cold ocean alternated between green and blue tinges, and the sun disappeared over the horizon, Mom, Dad and I began our ride back to Brantfield. Robin stayed home and watched over Brian and Doug.

I sat in the front seat and snuggled up to Mom. She held me close. Dad turned onto Atlantic Boulevard and we headed back to Brantfield. I felt a sadness deep inside me that intensified as we moved farther away from our new apartment, our new home. The weekend had been a tease. Mom and Dad said to keep my spirits up, that someday I would be able to stay at home again, and hopefully it would be soon. That night, as I lay in bed back in Brantfield, tears welled in the corners of my eyes and dropped onto my pillow as I thought about our new home. It had been such a long time that I had gotten used to being away. But now, I had renewed hope. I didn't get in any trouble all weekend. We had a new home and I felt like part of the family again. Maybe soon I wouldn't have to wait for Visiting Day. Maybe soon I would be able to stay at home, sleep in my own bed, play at the beach, go to school. Maybe soon I would be able to be part of the family again.

Mom wrote a poem about the ride back to Brantfield.

* * * *

At night on the long ride back
My coat is opened wide
And turning first this way, then that
He cuddles down inside.

His little arm around my waist
His head upon my breast
Its muted thump, the rise and fall
Lull sleepy lids to rest

And as he slumbers peacefully
Outside of where he first
Came to exist and stretched and moved
And grew,—then from me burst

Into the world of sound and space,
Squalling, red and freed

75

From the safe, warm, wet darkness
That fulfilled every need.

I with all my heart yearning
Pray that God will provide
For all the wants of my little boy
As He did, when he was inside.

* * * *

On Halloween day, Dr. Drake answered another one of Mom's letters. His support for Mom was evident; his grasp of my situation from afar was fading.

* * * *

October 31, 1962

Dear Mrs. Kane,

Many thanks for your letter.

I am most sorry to hear of your accident, and can appreciate how much having the continued problem with your leg reinforces your feeling depressed and wanting to give up the ghost. I can only hope you will continue to find the capacity to struggle on as you have, and that you will get started in treatment soon at the Evans Development Center.

The news about the children other than Troy is encouraging, especially Robin. Also Russ being in treatment now. I gather Troy continues to need hospitalization, though I can understand your feeling about how bleak and drab Brantfield

Mental Health Institute looks.

My best regards to the family, Russ and you.

Sincerely,

Matthew Drake, MD

* * * *

On the next Visiting Day, Mom said she had some exciting news. I hoped this meant I was coming home. Instead, she said we were moving from Ocean View Ave. to Chestnut Ave., which was only two streets over.

Mom said we were going to buy a house. It was going to be ours. We wouldn't have any landlord or other families living in the house with us. We were going to own it. I was happy, because we were still going to live near the beach. But I really lived in the Brantfield Mental Health Institute and not Belport, so I was also sad.

One afternoon, Charlie got all his stuff together. He was leaving Brantfield. I don't know if he went home or someplace else. Sometimes we got new kids on our ward and sometimes kids left. I had been there longer than a lot of the kids. I wondered when it would be my time to leave, to go home.

As Christmas got closer, I was excited. I could hardly wait for Santa to come. Mom and Dad said that I was going to be able to come home for Christmas. On Christmas day, we got up early and looked at our stockings first. There was candy and some small toys in my stocking. I got the chocolate coins I wanted. They looked like real money, but you could peel off the thin foil and eat them. We also opened our presents. I got some games and a baseball. It was fun playing with my presents, but I knew that I couldn't bring them back with me to Brantfield.

Later that day, we started moving our stuff from the apartment to our house on Chestnut Ave. The neighbors on our new street must have been staring out the window when we carried the Christmas tree with all our ornaments on it and the star at the top down Chestnut Ave. to our new house. But the excitement and joy of Christmas ended abruptly for me when I had to go back to Brantfield.

I didn't mark the date, but February was my one year anniversary at Brantfield. Things were changing in Belport, but my world stayed the same.

Mom was still not happy with the lack of treatment I got at Brantfield. She let Mr. Cummings know, and also complained to Dr. Jarrett and Dr. Culver about my discontinued therapy sessions. She felt that they weren't doing anything to help me get better. Despite Mom wanting to try to transfer me to the Crystal Home, the doctors at Brantfield did not agree and that talk had subsided.

I continued on this path, living in a mental institution. The screaming, yelling, strange behavior of the other kids became routine to me. Except for my family and Mr. Carlson, I didn't really have any friends. I just lived on the ward with the other kids who had problems.

As the summer approached, the doctors at Brantfield wanted to release me. Mom still wasn't sure. They hadn't given me the therapy sessions Dr. Drake had suggested. What if I came home and the same things started happening again? After discussions with Mr. Cummings, Mom felt she had assurances that if I had problems at home, Brantfield would readmit me.

In June, I graduated first grade from the Brantfield Mental Health Institute and received an honor medal for scholastic achievement. Mom said my teacher told her I was smart enough to skip second grade and go right to third. So I was coming home again. If all went well, I could again live with my family. I had spent the last year and a half incarcerated in a mental institution. It was the beginning of the summer. Soon I would turn seven.

6
Danger at Home

Tied into bed, unable to move,
You visit me in the morning light.
Feeling fear, pain, sadness, disgrace,
I look for clues in your face.

Humiliated, degraded, abused, almost death,
Is there something wrong with me?
You accuse, confuse, refuse to believe me,
Cruel punishment again, this time gasping for breath.

You say you love me, but can I trust you?
Trying to forget my hurt.
It is our secret that I keep,
There's something wrong with you, not me; I weep.

* * * *

Chestnut Ave. was a one-way road, with the beach's under-tow seemingly pulling traffic up the street towards Atlantic Boulevard and the ocean wall. There were single-family houses, two families and triple deckers, and even a small cottage that survived the influx of families into this crowded, coastal town. Chestnut Ave.

was middle class, filled with working parents and kids riding their bikes on the street and playing together.

The synagogue was within walking distance and served the Jewish families in the neighborhood. We went to 8 o'clock Sunday mass at the Saint Nicholas Church. Dad worked when everyone else was sleeping, getting the donuts, muffins and pastries ready for the early morning crowd. Saturday night was the only one during the week that Dad didn't have to work. He tried to stay up with Mom and watch TV, but he always fell asleep on the couch. When he got up early on Sunday morning to bring the family to church, Dad's throbbing head told him his body wanted to sleep, not get up. He took a few Extra Strength Anacins to lessen his headache.

Mom ironed our clothes in the parlor moments before we scurried out the door so we wouldn't be late for Sunday mass. We piled into the last row of the church, with Mom and Dad serving as bookends to make sure we weren't hitting each other, talking or laughing. I looked around at the people and all the statues, and quietly listened to the priest. Robin seemed to pay attention to what he said; Brian looked bored. Mom brought her index finger to her lips to signal to Doug to stop giggling.

Halfway through mass, Mom motioned to Robin, who was sitting next to Dad, to give him a nudge. He was sound asleep. Dad opened his eyes momentarily, but they signaled he was still tired. Robin woke him up again a few minutes later, but gave up after that and let Dad sleep. After mass, Dad bought donuts across the street from the church. They had really big honey dipped donuts.

When we got home, everyone got changed into regular clothes and we had breakfast. Dad read the sports page as he alternated between taking bites out of his donut and sipping coffee.

He said to no one in particular, "The Yankees look strong again this year. They have six guys on the All-Star team. The Red Sox have two, Yastrzemski and Monbouquette, the guy that pitched the no-hitter last year."

Mom asked me, "Troy, what do you want?"

"Can I have a honey-dipped?" I asked.

"You sure can. Here's a cold glass of milk, too," she added with a smile.

"Mantle made it too, but he broke his foot so he's out for a few months," Dad added.

When I came home from Brantfield that June, my family had already been living in Belport for 10 months. Robin had her friends from school and the neighborhood, like Betty who lived on Ocean View and Sandy from across the street. Brian played with Larry from around the corner on Davenport Road and sometimes Henry from the white double decker, and young Doug had Mom or Billy from the big green house. I wasn't used to making friends and playing with other kids; I had just stayed in the Rec room or climbed on the monkey bars at Brantfield, not making any real connections. But now I was the new kid on Chestnut Ave. in a neighborhood filled with kids and activity. I wondered if the other kids knew where I had been and why I had been away. I went outside and played, but pretty much kept to myself.

Although at times Mom didn't always seem happy with me, I made it through the summer without any major incidents. Mr. Cummings suggested that Mom enroll me in school in Belport. She was still a little hesitant about letting go of Brantfield, but she signed me up. So on August 31, 1963, I was officially released from Brantfield Mental Health Institute and could remain at home.

The very next week, I started second grade at the Roosevelt School. Robin was in the seventh grade, beginning Junior High at the center of town. Brian was in fourth grade, and Doug was just beginning pre-school, also at the Roosevelt School with me. The Roosevelt School was about a half-mile jaunt along Atlantic Boulevard and the sea wall. We weren't tall enough to see the ocean over the wall, until we got closer to where the wall morphed into a metal railing. You could see the entire beach from there, and the large tanker ships bobbing along on the horizon.

We had gone shopping for back-to-school clothes. I was proud to be wearing my own clothes instead of a mismatched, loose-fitting community wardrobe. I also got sneakers and a pair of shoes, which I was wearing as we walked that morning. Mom and Dad let me pick out my own shoes. I got light brown, suede shoes, and made sure I didn't scuff them on the sidewalk.

For a few moments, I forgot my nervousness of my first day at a regular school and worry that someone might know my secrets. The doctors and my teacher at Brantfield all said that I was smart, but I wasn't quite sure what to think. I wanted to be like the other kids, but I knew I was different. I was worried.

Mom helped us find our teachers and get into the right lines. Everyone was taller than me, even the girls. I tentatively waved goodbye as we headed in. With a last name that began with the letter K, my desk was sandwiched in the middle row. While the other kids joked and chatted, I longed for the comfort of my first grade class in Brantfield. My new teacher had us all write something about what we did in the summer.

I wrote about all the funs things I had done at the beach during the summer to amuse myself. My teacher collected our stories. She read a few of them out loud in front of the entire class. I really hoped my paper was hidden on the bottom of the pile. I already felt awkward enough; I didn't want everyone to be looking at me as she read about me going to the beach. Why did I write that? Of course everyone in Belport goes to the beach. We live right next to it. It's no big deal to them. I was relieved; she didn't read my paper out loud.

At recess time, we got to go outside. There weren't any monkey bars or swings like there were in Brantfield, but kids were running around and playing kickball and hanging around together on the paved schoolyard. A tall cyclone fence lined the outside of the jig-sawed property lines.

One of the kids kicked the ball off the side of his foot, and it hit the big, red chimney. I was standing alone next to the concrete plat-form near the chimney, and the ball ricocheted and almost hit me.

"Hey, throw it over here," called the boy who was the pitcher.

I picked it up and heaved it back towards him. It was a ball just like we used at Brantfield to play Bombardment and kick ball. I wanted to join the game, but nobody asked me to; so I watched. The rest of the morning went well. Mr. Cote, the principal, came into our class and introduced himself. With his solid white hair, horn-rimmed glasses and friendly smile, he seemed more like someone's doting grandfather instead of a principal. After school, I proudly showed Mom my spelling and penmanship papers.

Once a week, Mom, Dad and I had to go to the Evans Development Center. Each one of us went to a different psychia-trist. As I always did, I answered the doctor's questions and told him the history of the things I had done over the years. I told him how I did well at Brantfield, pleasing my teacher and not getting into any trouble with the counselors or other kids. When we first began our sessions, I was upbeat as things were going well for me since I had come home. However, my attitude, like the shorter days and tumbling leaves as summer turned to fal , quickly became more somber. Sometimes Robin, Brian and Doug came to Evans Development Center. They sat in the car, or walked around the building while Mom, Dad and I met with our psychiatrists. There wasn't a lot of stuff to do there, so other times they stayed home and Robin babysat.

Our house on Chestnut Ave. wasn't big, but I liked it a lot more than our apartment in Powell. When you first walked in, there was a bright, small room with a lot of windows. We called it the sun room. Then you had to step up to go into the parlor. It had a brick fireplace with a mantel. We didn't use the fireplace, but Mom had put a bellows and a black, metal shovel leaning up against it as decoration.

Heading straight back was the kitchen. We used a wooden picnic table with benches to seat our large family for meals. There were two built-in cabinets, one with glass doors that Mom used to show off her nice dishes and the other with a regular wood door that hid the canned goods, boxes of pasta and spices for cooking. There was an old sink with an open stack of shelves in the corner, with a small window overlooking the back yard. Off to the right was a French door leading to Mom and Dad's bedroom. Mom had applied solid paper adhesive sheets to block out the light from the kitchen and give them privacy.

Since Dad took a nap after supper before he worked all night, we couldn't make noise and had to stay out of the kitchen in the evening. Upstairs were two bedrooms and the bathroom. Robin had one of the bedrooms, and Brian, me and Doug shared the back bedroom, which had a sloping ceiling forming an upside down V. It was hot in there in the summer. We didn't get any breeze through the window leading out to the angled roof and back yard.

About a week after school began, some of the old problems started up again. At first, it wasn't too bad. Mom said she noticed something in the house, I think it was tattered wallpaper in the living room, and asked me if I had torn it. She said there was also writing on the painted woodwork. I told her I didn't do it. She didn't seem angry.

Then, she started asking me in the morning when I woke up if I had gotten up in the middle of the night. I was sure I hadn't, but she didn't believe me. One morning, she told Robin, Brian and Doug to go to school. Mom told me to stay in my room. She didn't yell, but I could tell she was fuming.

Dad hadn't come home from work yet. The front door opened and closed as Robin, Brian and Doug headed off to school. I heard

Mom's determined steps creaking up the wooden stairs, faster than usual. I sat frozen on the edge of my bed, waiting for the bedroom door to open, trying to hold back my fear. I knew I was in trouble. Mom came in and closed the door behind her. It felt like the slanted walls and narrow ceiling pulled in closer. There was no place to hide; I couldn't run. Why didn't Mom let me go to school? I knew she would want answers and I knew I wouldn't have them.

"Troy, did you get up last night in the middle of the night?" she began.

"No Mom," I quickly answered.

"Are you sure?"

"No Mom. I mean ya I'm sure," I said.

"Troy, tell me the truth."

"I am. I stayed in bed all night," I said.

In all the time I had been at Brantfield, Mr. Carlson never asked me what I had done when everyone was sleeping. Dr. Culver never asked me. Nobody at Brantfield ever yelled at me or punished me. In that instant, sitting on my bed, it felt like I was back in Powell with Mom asking me questions about what I did and getting mad at me. Maybe it would be different this time. Maybe Mom would believe me. I hated wondering what was going to happen next. All I could do was wait. I was frightened.

"What did you do last night when you got up?" she continued.

"I didn't do anything," I said, trying to say it in a nice voice so I wouldn't make her mad.

She changed the questions around a little as she pressed me for details, trying to throw me off and get me to admit my guilt, but she wasn't able to trick me this time. I kept saying that I didn't get up and do anything. Like a prosecutor unable to crack the key witness, Mom's irritation became noticeable. After one more denial, she couldn't take it any longer and she suddenly reacted. She grabbed me by the arm and started swinging as she spun me around. She hit me with rapid fire slaps, anywhere she could reach across my back and upper legs as I tried to spin and duck out of the way.

"Don't you lie to me," she said with authority in her voice.

She hit me and hit me and hit me. Harder and harder. Not only did each whack sting, but I could tell she was out of control, like a volcano suddenly exploding and then spewing hot lava after years of inactivity. I cried from pain, fear and hurt inside. Why was she doing this? What did I do?

"I'm sorry, I'm sorry, Mom. Please, please," I pleaded.

When Mom was finally physically and emotionally spent, she stopped. She breathed heavy. I tried to stop crying. As the physical pain lessened, I was left feeling humiliated and scared. Mom composed herself; there was an awkward silence.

I glanced at her to check if we were done. No, we weren't. Even though she was now under control, I could tell she was still too mad at me to stop. She rested for another long, silent pause. Like the moments before an impending ocean storm pelts the coast, there was an eerie calmness as I waited for her next strike.

She began questioning again. I figured it would be safer this time to admit anything that she said. I told her I did get up during the night. But it was never that easy. She still wanted me to tell her what I did, exactly what I did. Why did I have to say what I did if she already knew it? I would have said whatever she wanted me to say. I just didn't know the right words. I tried, but I couldn't get it right. I never could. She said I was lying. I knew I was lying, but I was trying to say the lie she wanted me to say. Mom didn't have patience for my fumbling attempts, and she unleashed a second attack, her anger more fierce this time.

More hits, more pain. As she hit the areas she had already hit during the first episode, it brought back the first pain and then added more to it. She didn't go on as long this time. She didn't have to. I was punished. We were done. Mom walked out of the room.

The next day I went to school. I ran and played tag at lunch. I was quicker than a lot of the other kids. Usually they couldn't catch me, but towards the end of recess one of the kids tagged me. Now I was it. I tagged most of the kids and brought them back to the jail, which was the big chimney. I chased after Frank, one of the faster boys. He shifted right and then left, and I stayed with him. Then he stopped and slid behind one of the girls, who we didn't notice until the last second.

I quickly turned to avoid running into her. My foot slid out from under me. I fell on the hard pavement, tearing my pants and cutting my knee. Frank stopped running and a few kids gathered around me to see if I was okay. It hurt a lot, but I was able to hold back my tears. One of the teachers took me to see the school nurse.

"Looks like you got a good scrape there, Troy," the nurse said.

"Ya," I said softly.

While she was cleaning up the cut and putting a bandage on it, Mr. Cote walked in.

"You're a brave boy, Troy. Do you play baseball?" he asked.

"Yes, sir," I said quietly.

"Then you can probably use this," he said.

Mr. Cote handed me a brand new baseball. The sparkling white rawhide was held tightly together by the red stitching. It even had *Major League* printed on it.

My problems seemed to be getting worse. Mom punished me for a lot of things. She also punished Brian. Sometimes rather than hitting him, she would tickle him. Brian didn't like it. At first, he laughed and squirmed. Weighing 100 or more pounds than Brian, she was able to hold him down. Eventually, he got really mad and started crying.

Mom also used the black, metal fireplace shovel sometimes instead of spanking us with her hands. It really hurt. And a few times when she said I got up at night and did things, Mom brought me down to the kitchen, and pulled out the black pepper. She filled up a teaspoon until it was overflowing.

"Now swallow all of it," she demanded.

After the first time, I knew what to expect.

"Please, Mom. I'll be good."

"Open wide," she said.

She put the spoon in my mouth. I dutifully got it all off the spoon and swallowed it. I knew it would be worse for me if I didn't obey her. Like a brush fire spreading wildly, I felt the burn work its way up through my nostrils and down my throat and to my stomach. My eyes watered. The taste was overwhelming. After a few minutes, she let me drink water, which helped a little but it also seemed to intensify the burn and the foul taste.

Mom wanted to stop me from getting up at night, so she asked Dad to put a lock on our bedroom door. Dad screwed in a slide-bolt lock to the top part of the door. From the hallway, you could slide the bolt to connect the door with the door frame, and keep it closed, or do the reverse to unlock and open it. From inside the room, you could jiggle the door a little, but you couldn't open it, and it would make a lot of noise if you tried. At night, after Brian, Doug and I went to bed, Mom would lock the door.

"Troy, I want to talk to you," Mom said a few mornings after the lock was in place.

Panic set in. What had I done now? What was she going to do?

Mom came in the bedroom and closed the door. She began her interrogation.

I knew I didn't do anything because the room was locked all night. I couldn't have done anything. Mom wanted to know how I opened the door during the night. And if I said I hadn't unlocked the door, then I knew she would get angrier. And of course, she wanted me to tell her what I had done after I got up and unlocked the door, without giving me any clues. No matter what I said,

Mom didn't believe me. She got frustrated and hit me and pun-ished me.

I tried hard in school, but I was really struggling. I hated to read in front of the other kids, because it felt like they were all looking at me. It took me longer to read than the other kids, and I fumbled some of the words. It was the same with the other subjects too. I never got in any trouble, but the school papers I brought home showed I wasn't doing well.

One week, we all went to Evans Development Center. After the therapy session, we walked around Mason Heights Park. It was crowded and people walked along the hardtop paths, or sat on benches or fed the squirrels and pigeons.

As we walked back to the car, we noticed a joke shop and went in. Dad showed us some funny things, like the fart cushion, the handshake buzzer and the flower that sat in your sport coat lapel and squirted water at people when you squeezed the rubber sack, or the chewing gum that tasted really bad.

Mom didn't seem interested in this funny stuff. When we were ready to go, Dad let us get a few things and Mom got some plas-tic handcuffs. That night when I was going to bed, Mom put the handcuffs on me and explained that this would prevent me from wandering around the house in the middle of the night.

She used the plastic keys to lock them on my wrists. Then she threaded her old nylon stockings through the handcuffs and se-cured them to the frame of the bed. Before she tied the knots, she made sure I could move my hands a little from side-to-side, but not enough to try to take them off or untie the nylon knots. Mom seemed lost in the detail of making this secure.

The handcuffs fit loosely around my wrists, but I couldn't take them off. It was a strange feeling having to wear handcuffs and be-ing tied into bed. As I laid there on my back, my nose felt itchy. Instinctively, I tried to scratch it, but the nylon constraints stopped my hands. I was able to push my body towards the foot of the bed and move my hands up to my face, and reach my nose. I felt a sense of relief as my fingernails relieved my itch.

The next morning, I heard the now familiar noise of Mom unlocking the door to our room. The floor was covered with dirty clothes, discarded from the prior days' use. It was different from when we lived in Powell, where Mom made sure the apartment was spotless. In our new home, she didn't keep up with the smelly sheets and dirty clothes, piled on the cellar stairs waiting to be washed.

As Mom came over to me, I felt instant relief as her expression said that I wasn't in trouble. She untied the knots and released the nylons. Then she put the key in the handcuff lock, and turned it. The handcuff sprung open. I was free and could get out of bed and get ready for school.

A few mornings later when Mom unlocked our bedroom door and briskly entered, her stern look foretold a very different scenario. Brian and Doug got dressed for school, and then went down to eat breakfast. Mom didn't untie the nylon knots that held me in place. She didn't unlock the handcuffs to free my hands. Robin, Brian and Doug went off to school.

I waited for Mom to return. Finally she entered the room and closed the door. I nervously awaited my fate.

"I don't know if you did it before you went to bed, or after, but you got up again last night," she said.

"I'm sorry, Mom," I said compliantly.

"I want you to tell me what you did, Troy," she said.

The story played out about the same, with me trying to guess what I should say, and Mom getting madder and madder at me as I made up lies trying to please her. She began spanking me. The pain was awful, and still being tied into bed and not being able to move made it even worse. I'm not sure I could have done anything to defend myself, but it was frightening not being able to use my hands at all.

I kept to myself at school, not making many friends. I knew I wasn't doing well in my subjects, and it made me feel worse. Maybe part of it was because the school I attended at the Brantfield Mental Health Institute wasn't a real school. I am not sure, but after hearing about my high IQ for several years, doing poorly put another dent in my confidence. After school, I came right home and usually went up to our bedroom. I didn't go out and play with the neighborhood kids.

One afternoon after school, while sitting alone on my bed, I heard Dad coming up the stairs. He always had that upbeat trot whenever he went up and down the stairs. He didn't have to say anything. I knew instantly it was him. Even though I felt sad and alone, seeing Dad come into the room brought out a little smile in me.

"What are you doing, Troy?" he asked.

"Nothing," I answered.

"You know, there are a lot of kids on our street. It is a nice day. I bet you would have fun going outside and playing with them," he said.

I knew he was trying to be nice. He wouldn't make me go out and play if I didn't want to. He just wanted me to have some fun. But I didn't feel like being with other people. I didn't know the other kids. I didn't feel like trying to make new friends.

"I know," I said.

"You won't know what you are missing if you don't give it a try." Dad persisted.

I knew he was right, but I didn't want to be with anybody else, especially kids that I didn't know.

"Ya," I said like I was agreeing to the dentist pulling out one of my teeth.

A few mornings later, lying on my back, I waited in bed for Mom. Robin, Brian and Doug were already up and on their way to school. Mom had stopped using the handcuffs, instead tying the nylons directly around my wrists and ankles and securing them to the frame of the bed.

It all seemed like a bad dream that never ended. Tied into bed at night. Interrogated in the morning. No memory of doing these bad things. Feeling like there was something wrong with me that I couldn't control. No matter how hard I tried to be good and please Mom, things always came pointing back to me.

Little did I know that this morning was going to be different and more memorable from anything that I had ever experienced. It started out like many other mornings before it. I was scared and trying to think of what I was going to say.

Mom came into the bedroom, my inner antennae trying to sense her mood and how I should act. She seemed the same at first, but she must have already been very frustrated. When my answers to her questions were not what she wanted to hear, her anger skyrocketed. There weren't going to be a lot of questions. She was mad and I was her target. She didn't hit me. Instead she grabbed the pillow and covered my face with it. Instinctively, I went to push it away with my hands, but they were restrained. I tried to grab the pillow, but I couldn't get close to reaching it. I panicked, twisting and turning my head as I tried to get out from under the pillow and her grasp. It was like a coffin lid suddenly closing on me. She pushed harder on the pillow, and my face sunk deep into the pillow case, covering up my mouth and nostrils.

I wasn't getting any air. I tried to scream, but I couldn't.

I dug my heals into the mattress and tried to arch my back and hopefully wiggle free. Like someone sinking into quicksand, it was hard to move. I'm not sure how much Mom weighed at the time, but my guess is somewhere between 175 and 200 pounds. She pressed her weight against me to hold down my legs and arms. My oxygen was running out. I frantically tried harder and harder to get free, but she had me pinned. I needed to do something quick. She wouldn't let me breathe.

It was horrifying. It was like being held at the bottom of the pool, and not being able to swim to the top and get air. She wouldn't let me move. My breath ran out. "Please! Please! Help me! Help me!" I thought, but couldn't say.

But there wasn't anyone there to help. It was just Mom and me. There was no air. I had never felt like this before. It was like my head was going to explode. I kept trying to fight back, but a horrible sensation was taking over my body. I think I was losing consciousness.

I was going to die.

Then, Mom took the pillow off my face. I gasped for air. At first, my lungs couldn't catch up. I gulped the air with deep breaths. I was going to live, but I was shocked. Mom had smothered me, held me down and put a pillow over my face. She almost killed me. And she did it on purpose.

I wanted to get as far away from her as I could, but I was still tied into bed and at her mercy.

She took a minute to compose herself, and then she calmly said, "Troy, now I know you got up last night. I want you to tell me what you did."

Oh my god. She wasn't finished. She was going to smother me again if I didn't come up with something quickly, or if I couldn't make her like me enough to let me go. I tried not to cry because it might make her mad, but I couldn't help it. I thought, somebody please help me. I hoped Dad would come home from work right then, and save me.

But nobody helped. It was just me and her. She sat on the side of the bed, close enough to quickly cut off my air again. She had less patience for my visible fear and wrong answers. I knew she was going to strike again. I began to try to move my body and head so she wouldn't be able to thrust the pillow over my mouth and nose. It worked for a moment, but then she put her right hand over my mouth and closed off my nostrils with her left hand. Her weight once again wedged me in place.

I tried to scream, but it was muffled. Nobody could hear me. I fought as hard as I could, but I didn't have the breath or the energy to last long and my hands and feet were still tightly tied to the bed frame. I felt like I was sinking into the depths of the ocean, with no air or light. I am not sure if I passed out, but everything was dark. Then she stopped.

Air began flowing in and out of me. My body started working again. Mom untied me. She said something to me, but I didn't hear a word of it. I was shattered. My mother had almost killed me.

7
Home Is Not Home

Adults that abuse children, instill fear, shame and helplessness in their victims. Children, if they have a relationship with the abuser, may feel responsible for the abuse, a sense of loyalty to the abuser, and blame themselves for what they get. The children may hang onto the belief that they have some sense of control; that if they act differently, they won't get abused. However, the triggers for the abuse may not be consistent and are not controlled by the victim. So even if these children want to change their behavior to avoid further abuse, they cannot stop it.

To try to maintain themselves and survive in the face of this horror, abused children use a variety of coping mechanisms. They may comply with the abuser, they may fight back, they may tell lies, they may try to improve their relationship with the abuser, and anything else they can come up with. Lacking in self-confidence as they suffer torture and humiliation, they also may retreat from others. And sadly, they may turn inward and keep the secret of their abuse to themselves. While these coping mechanisms and patterns for survival may somehow get them through it, rebuilding their sense of self and forming relationships with others may become a daunting, lifelong challenge. No matter what, if they survive the abuse, their lives will never be the same.

* * * *

After Mom smothered me, I was in a state of shock. She had tied me into bed to keep me from getting up in the middle of the night, but then smothered me until I ran out of breath. I was defenseless. It was like someone had buried me alive, and I was unable to inhale as the dirt filled my lungs. I panicked. I feverishly tried to kick and push and scream, but it was hopeless. The nylons were tied into tight knots around my wrists and ankles and secured to the frame of the bed. Mom leaned on me and pinned me down. I couldn't breathe or move. My time was running out. I knew it and I felt it.

This wasn't an accident. She didn't get mad, react and slap me in the face, only to apologize. She had blocked my mouth and nose, first with a pillow and then with her own hands. She intentionally wouldn't let me breathe, and she didn't stop. As she held her hand firmly across my mouth, and squeezed my nostrils together with her fingers, she had to see the terror in my eyes, and my struggle to survive. I couldn't understand how my mother could intentionally make me suffer like this.

Once she started smothering me, there was no turning back. I don't know how long it lasted, but it seemed like forever. She went long past the point of me not being able to hold my breath. I was close to losing consciousness, maybe worse, and she deliberately imposed this on me.

It was such a horrible, frightening feeling. Any time I thought about it after that, it felt like it was happening all over again. My heart pounded, my breathing raced and my mind felt the frenzied attempts to get free and gulp air once again. It was like I could almost step outside of myself and watch. I couldn't stop going over it in my mind, reliving the terror over and over again.

When she came in to question me in the morning, she had to unlock the door first and then untie me. How could I have done

96

anything? How could I have untied my hands and legs, and then unlocked the door from inside the bedroom? How could I have escaped out of the room, done something wrong, then gone back inside the bedroom, slid the bolt on the outside of the door even though I was on the inside, and then tied myself back into bed?

I was just a second grader, but I knew it didn't make sense. I didn't know what to do. I didn't say anything to anyone. Not Robin, nor Brian. Doug was too young, but I wouldn't have told him either. Somehow I always held out hope that Dad would come home from work and save me. It always happened when he was not home, and I knew he wouldn't let it happen if he we there. Despite the terrifying impact it had on me, I never said anything to Dad either. In fact, I never said anything to Dad at any point in my life about what had happened. For some reason, I silently dealt with this trauma, alone.

Somehow, I didn't stop loving Mom. She was my mother. She was involved with everything in my life. But from then on, I was afraid of her and didn't trust her. Anytime after that first smothering incident, whenever she tied me into bed at night, I wanted to jump out of bed and run while I still could. I wanted to tell her that it wasn't me doing all these things, and convince her once and for all. Instead, I lay on my back and kept still as she tied the nylons. I held my hands and legs in place for her so she could tie me securely into bed. I knew I had lost any hope of protecting myself, and worried that I might have to go through more torture again the next morning.

And yet, there was this other feeling inside me that wondered if I did the things Mom said I did and that was why I was getting punished. When I thought back, I had no memories of these acts, but I guess I still wondered if somehow I did what she said I did but didn't know it. Mom was so sure when she told me the things I had done. She also confidently went through the entire history with every doctor we met. I could recite the history, which I often did to answer doctors' questions. I said the words, but I didn't feel emotion or remorse because these weren't my memories.

I forgot or blocked out other parts of the history. When Mom brought them up to the psychiatrists, some things made me feel uncomfortable or just seemed wrong.

It felt like being in a strange dream where things are not the way they should be, but I followed the rules even though I didn't want to. It didn't make sense to me, and the smothering made the consequences of what I sometimes admitted to doing severe. But if I didn't come up with exact details for Mom, then she got just as mad at me, and punished me anyway. I was entangled in her web and just trying to survive.

Many nights, after Mom kissed Brian, me and Doug good night, turned out the lights and slid the outside latch on the door after leaving, I would lie in bed, surrounded by my stuffed animals, wondering what was in store for me in the morning. With an internal alarm clock that sensed imminent danger, I woke up early each morning, before she came upstairs. Still tied into bed, I wondered if I had done something in the middle of the night and if she would be mad at me. When she came into our bedroom, she didn't have to tell me with words if I was in trouble. I knew right away. In fact, I could usually tell by how she walked up the stairs and unlocked the door what was going to happen.

A few days after the first smothering incident, it happened again. She went through the usual questions, and she was getting angry. The pace of her questions quickened and her veiled calm demeanor was wearing thin. I knew it was coming. I wasn't courageous; I was petrified as I prepared myself to go through it again. With each question, my panic increased. I tried to stall her as long as I could, admitting to things I might have done wrong, and describing how I did them. Answering questions, but not really answering them while trying hard not to make her angry.

I would have swallowed the whole container of black pepper, or let her hit me as long as she wanted to if she would have agreed to not smother me again. But it wasn't up to me. When the interrogations began, my heart sank. I knew it was hopeless. She was going to smother me. If instant death was a choice, I might have picked it rather than suffer the fear, anxiety and pain surrounding being smothered while tied into bed and feeling like I was dying and not being able to do anything about it.

There were other signs that things were not going well. When we lived in Powell, Mom made sure the apartment was spotless, but our house in Belport was really messy. The counters in the kitchen were cluttered with stuff, which only seemed to grow over time. There were clothes all over the floor in our bedroom. The stairs in the basement became a dumping ground for dirty clothes, and the pile grew and grew. Trying to go down the basement stairs was a lot like climbing over a snow bank in the middle of winter.

She didn't tell me, but by October, Mom was actively trying to get me back into an institution. She called Mr. Cummings at Brantfield, but they wouldn't take me back. Like before, most places had long waiting lists or didn't handle kids like me. Despite Mom's emotional pleas for help at a number of places she called, her efforts failed. I remained at home with no real prospects of getting admitted anywhere in the near future.

On the morning of Thursday, November 1, Mom's pace was quick as she climbed the stairs, unlocked the bedroom door and entered. She woke Brian and Doug. Brian went downstairs to have breakfast and go off to school, but she wanted Doug and me to stay in the room.

She was holding a hammer in her hands. She put the hammer down on the dresser and went over to Doug. She wanted to know if he was okay. She began checking his head. Doug said he was okay. Mom hugged him and began asking him questions. Her intensity scared him and me. She wanted to know if I had hit him in the head with the hammer.

Doug said that I hadn't. He looked nervous.

Then she asked me if I had hit Doug with the hammer. I immediately said no. I didn't hold back my reaction this time. With fear in my voice, like so many times before, I repeated myself saying no I didn't do it.

Mom said that she had found the hammer on the counter in the kitchen, instead of in the basement with Dad's tools like it should have been. Doug seemed to be okay. She took the hammer and went downstairs with Doug, leaving me tied in bed. She came back upstairs a little later and said that Doug had said that I had hit him in the head with the hammer.

I was in big trouble.

Mom untied me and told me to get washed up and dressed, and to stay in my room. A little later, I heard the front door open, and then Mom telling Dad about me hitting Doug in the head with his hammer. I heard Dad talking to Doug, making sure he was okay. Then I heard Dad coming upstairs to see me. The wooden stairs didn't have much chance to creak as he rapidly climbed the stairs, two at a time.

My stomach churned as I waited. Dad came in and wanted to know why I had hit Doug in the head with a hammer. I mumbled that I didn't do it, that I didn't remember anything about it. Dad said that I could have killed Doug. I felt ashamed, and could tell that Dad was really disappointed in me. It was one more incident in a long series of incidents that I had done. Dad seemed to be on my side sometimes, even if he didn't always say so, but this time he was really upset. I almost wished that Dad had spanked me. I felt awful.

Mom and Dad took me to the Emergency Clinic at Mason Heights Children's Center. Mom told the doctor about how I got the hammer from the basement and hit Doug in the head with it. No one had witnessed it, but Doug had confirmed that I hit him in the head with the hammer while he was sleeping. Mom said that it wasn't safe having me at home with the other kids, especially my younger brother, Doug.

I sat quietly and listened to Mom go into detail. I felt ashamed, confused and alone. Then the doctor turned to me, and asked me about what had happened. I told him that I didn't remember any of it. He must have thought I was lying. I wanted to hide my face, which felt hot and flushed.

The Medical Report from Children's Center summarized the emergency clinic visit.

* * * *

Medical Emergency Clinic
November 1, 1963

Odd, sad story. Patient took hammer to head of younger sibling during latter's sleep last night.

Patient at Brantfield Mental Health Institute 1/62 - 6/63. Released and parents told he was not psychotic, would not be given outpatient care there. They have been trying Evans Development Center. Has frequently threatened his two brothers to death, bangs head frequently, and last night struck 5 year old sibling with hammer on head, but denied any knowledge of this. Parents do not feel they can care for child at <u>home</u> any longer.

** Patient had several seizures witnessed only by siblings !!

Never seen by parents, but once corroborated by neighbor!

Neurological Note
Seen in Medical Emergency Clinic. Story of hitting brother with hammer last evening (not proved but brother states incident occurred and mother states hammer was downstairs but not in proper place).

Patient's denial is given in a low voice and with head hanging. Would not even talk about incident, claiming no memory at all of what happened. Hallucinations in patient history not typical of temporal lobe halluci-nations. Past EEGs and inpatient workups negative for any organic neurological disorder.

Physical exam-Detailed neurological exam performed-no abnormalities found.

Impression-Not a seizure disorder. Parents receiving psychiatric care. Boy should have benefit of psychi-atric evaluation before he is abandoned. Seemed to do better when he was cared for by clinic here.

Will have patient return to Neurological clinic next week and at that time request opinion of psychiatrist as to whether patient can be carried on outpatient basis therapy or whether he needs inpatient care.

RX for meprobamate 250 mg each evening given until clinical appointment.

* * * *

When I returned to Children's Center the next week, not much happened. Either they did not think I needed to be admitted somewhere, or they could not arrange it. I don't know. However, I remained at home.

The middle of the night problems escalated. Mom was convinced that rather than trying to get out of the locked bedroom door, I instead crawled out the bedroom window onto the roof in the middle of the night. From there, she said I had walked around the roof and tore up some of the shingles. Then I came back through the window into the bedroom, and got back into bed and tied myself back in.

I didn't think I did the other things she said I did. At least most of the time I didn't believe it. But I didn't see how I could have climbed up on the roof in the dark and not remembered anything about it. But Mom was sure that I had done it. I had to swallow heaping spoonfuls of black pepper a few times as punishment. It burned my nostrils, mouth and throat, but at least I could breathe.

Mom said how dangerous it was to go out on the roof. So she had Dad hammer nails into the only window in our bedroom so that I could not open it. And yet, Mom interrogated me about going out on the roof even after Dad had nailed the window shut. In that bedroom, her questions were real, with tough consequences waiting at the other end of my responses.

Maybe it was because I was getting older, or maybe I was starting to see through some of the stories that didn't make sense to me. Whatever the reason, I was sure that I hadn't done at least some of the things that Mom said I did. She continued to repeat the same claims and more, as my history for my visits to psychiatrists and social workers grew.

One day after school, Mom lost control of her temper. I was in my bedroom and in trouble because she said I had gone out on the roof the night before. Frustrated, she grabbed a metal clothes hanger and began hitting me with it. The metal from the hanger whacked against my arms as I instinctively put them up to shield myself. As she connected, the pain stung my hands and forearms, leaving welts that quickly became bruises.

When I went to school the next day, I had black and blue marks on my hands and arms from the beating. I'm not sure if my teacher sent me to the nurse or how I ended up seeing her, but when I got there, the nurse asked what had happened to me. Maybe it was because it felt good to be able to tell her, or maybe it was because I was used to telling grownups things that were bad, but I told her matter-of-factly that my mother had hit me with a clothes hanger because she thought I had climbed out on the roof.

The nurse was very surprised at my story. She asked me more questions to find out what happened. I repeated what I had said. I wasn't sure if she believed me or if she thought I was making it up. When I got home, Mom was waiting for me as I came into the sun room. Her expression was all business. There would be no idle chat about what I had done during school, or looking at any of my school papers.

"What did you tell the nurse at school today?" she asked in a serious tone.

My heart sank.

"I told her that I got punished for going out on the roof," I answered.

"Well, the nurse told me that you said I had hit you and caused the bruises you have. You know that you got those bruises from climbing out on the roof and falling. I heard you out there," she explained.

I knew I didn't go out on the roof and I knew she had hit me with the clothes hanger. I didn't disagree or say anything. I knew she was already mad that I had said something at school about it, but this time felt different from other times when I was in trouble. She made it clear that I didn't have my story right, that what I said wasn't true. But she was the one lying. She could say what she wanted to, but I was positive what had happened in the middle of the afternoon when I was awake and I had the black and blues to prove it.

Mrs. Jordan worked at the Roosevelt School as a psychologist. She had already been talking with Mom before the incident with the nurse. Mom must have explained the situation to the nurse and Mrs. Jordan, because I never heard anything else about it. Mom talked to Mrs. Jordan about my situation and getting me proper care. She became an ally to Mom, trying to do whatever she could to give her support.

Even though I was not put in an institution after the hammer incident with Doug, Mom was working hard to get me admitted someplace that had therapy as a treatment option. She called and wrote the Director of the Evans Development Center, telling about my long, frustrating history, and recent dangerous episode with the hammer. The Director spoke with Dr. Malone, the head of the Juvenile Unit at Evans Development Center about my case.

Before Thanksgiving, Dr. Malone contacted Mom and scheduled an appointment to have me evaluated. Dr. Malone concluded that he would not see me in the Juvenile Unit as an outpatient, unless I lived somewhere other than my current home.

In December, Mom spoke with Mrs. Maltin, the Director of Child Guardianship. She didn't feel that I could be placed in a foster home, because my history of violence made me a threat to the other kids in the home. So she would try to find a group home to place me in. However, she estimated it could take anywhere from a year to 18 months.

I'm not sure where the idea originated, but my mother became aware of a possible solution. If my parents brought me to court as a stubborn child, then the court would decide if I needed psychiatric help, and if I did, they would make sure I got treatment. The only catch was that my parents had to give up custody of me. This meant that the State would be responsible for me and my care. Initially, Mom didn't want to do this.

In early January, Mrs. Jordan, the school psychologist, visited us at home. She suggested that Mom and Dad talk to Dr. Malone again, but maybe the Stubborn Child option was the best approach. Mom wrote a letter to Dr. Drake, asking for his advice. He responded with the following letter.

* * * *

January 31, 1964

Dear Mrs. Kane,

I was sorry to hear about the return of Troy's severe emotional difficulties. I can well imagine how heartbreaking and at times overwhelming this whole situation is. However, I am sure Russ and you are talking this thing over with your doctors at the Evans Development Center.

If you will pardon my commenting at long distance about one specific area of your difficulties, even though I am not aware of the current details. I think the issue you must face and review again, if you haven't, is the need for Troy to live away from you for the present regardless of whether he is able to get therapy right away or not. He clearly was unable to maintain his emotional gains from hospitalization this fall and apparently Dr. Jarrett doesn't feel a further period of hospitalization at Brantfield is what Troy needs. To avoid considering the possibility of foster home placement, if this is at all manageable, where Troy might settle down, would be doing your whole family and you a disservice. I would urge you to review this ~~situation~~ question with your doctor again. To make foster home place-ment contingent upon Troy getting therapy isn't in anybody's best interests.

Thank you for your letter. My best regards to Russ, Troy, the family and you.

Sincerely yours,

Matthew Drake, MD

* * * *

Mom spoke with Dr. Malone, and he agreed the quickest way to get me the care I needed was probably through a court order. So Mom and Dad decided to bring me to the Scottboro District Court as a Stubborn Child. Mrs. Jordan worked with the Belport Police Chief to make the arrangements. After spending seven rough months at home, I was leaving again.

8
Ward of the State

In 1646, the General Court of Massachusetts Bay passed the Stubborn Child law, making it a capital offense for children to disobey their parents and outlined the recourse that parents had. The law was based on the wording in the Deuteronomy, the fifth book of the Bible. The law stated that a child, 16 years of age or older, who did not obey his mother or father could be put to death by the State. In 1654, the Massachusetts Stubborn Child Act established that a father could petition the court regarding his stubborn child to put the child to death. Fortunately, this never happened. Similar Stubborn Child laws were also put into effect in Connecticut (1650), Rhode Island (1668) and New Hampshire (1679). These laws were indicative of the attitude that children were to be controlled and did not have the rights that adults had.

In 1866, Henry Bergh, who had founded the Society for the Prevention of Cruelty to Animals to ensure proper treatment of dogs and cats, brought a case to the Supreme Court of a child who was beaten cruelly by her custodians. The case received much publicity and resulted in establishing the similar organization for children, the Prevention of Cruelty to Children. By the 1970s, the Stubborn Child law had changed significantly.

* * * *

It was March, 1964. Mom bought me a little blue suitcase because I was going away. I had never had my own suitcase. I loved the light blue color. When positioned on its side, the suitcase had a footprint about the size of a placemat you put on the table for dinner. It was deep enough to hold two of my stuffed animals, laying on their sides. When I picked it up by the plastic handle, I felt like a big kid. While intended more for a child's overnight stay at his or her grandparents' house, it held my toothpaste, toothbrush, pajamas, and stuffed animal, Buddy.

"What a winner," Dad said as a car cut in front of us in the traffic logjam. Dad slowly worked his way through it and let us off in front of the Scottboro District courthouse because we were almost late. Mom and I rushed into the building and told the woman at the desk that we were there. Dad caught up with us a few minutes later. After a while, a uniformed bailiff came into the waiting room and told us to come into the courtroom. He directed us to have a seat at a big table at the front of the room. I hopped up on one of the wooden chairs. My feet dangled in the air as the bailiff announced the case to the judge, who proclaimed loudly that Troy Kane was charged with being a stubborn child by his parents, Russ and Brenda Kane.

The judge peered over his eyeglasses at me. He was an older man, adorned in black robes. I meekly glanced up at him. As he read over a few papers in front of him, the awkward silence seemed to last forever. I wondered if he was going to yell at me.

He finally began. "Good morning Mr. and Mrs. Kane and Troy. The law states that a stubborn child is one who 'stubbornly refuses to submit to the lawful and reasonable commands of a parent or guardian.' In other words, the child must, within reason, follow the rules of the house."

"You have brought Troy here this morning with the complaint that he is a Stubborn Child. For the record, Mr. or Mrs. Kane, can you tell the court about the situation you have been dealing with regarding your son, Troy?"

Mom stood up and started, "Well, your honor, first of all, Troy is a good little boy, but he is ill. This is a very hard thing for my husband, Russ, and I to do."

She was very emotional and fought to hold back her tears.

The judge said, "Take your time."

"Well, Troy was always a bright boy and very active. He could be stubborn sometimes, but was usually well behaved. Then about two years ago, Troy became very jealous of his siblings and started to be destructive, especially at night. One time, we couldn't find one of the sharp kitchen knives, because Troy had taken it. We didn't know what he was going to do. The kids and all of us were scared. In November, Troy got a hammer out of the basement and hit his five-year old brother, Doug, in the head with it during the night."

Mom's voice began to crack as she started to cry.

"What happened to the brother?"

"Doug didn't want to admit that Troy had hit him with the hammer. Fortunately, Doug is all right. I brought Troy to Mason Heights Children's Center and they admitted him, but they couldn't keep him there. After making a lot of phone calls and writing letters to the Director of Evans Development Center, they agreed to evaluate Troy. Dr. Malone said that they could treat Troy but not while he lived at home. They had a long waiting list and couldn't admit Troy at that time. Dr. Malone suggested that we bring Troy to court as a Stubborn Child, and he promised that he would work with Troy if we could get the court to admit him."

"I've tried every other way to get Troy into the right place that could give him the treatment he needs. It has been very frustrating

and hard for the family. We love Troy and don't want to lose custody of him, but this is the only way we can get him the help he
needs. So we brought Troy here today so he can get therapy and
then come back home to us someday."

"Well, Mrs. Kane, you and your husband should be commended
for doing something that is obviously very difficult in hopes of helping your son, Troy. It also sounds like a dangerous situation. Before
the State can decide the best placement for Troy, it must conduct a
full psychological evaluation. Therefore, I am going to continue this
case for 30 days until such time as the evaluation is completed, and
then the State can arrange the proper treatment for your son."

I wasn't really sure what all this meant. Mom seemed relieved.
Dad was quiet and had a blank look on his face. Then it began to
sink in. I was not going home.

A man in a suit came over to us and introduced himself and said
he was from the Youth Development Council. He said we could say
our goodbyes and then I would be going with him to the Mill Valley
Detention Center, where I would be evaluated.

My eyes began to well up. I didn't want to go away. Mom held
me tight and cried. Dad hugged me and then put his hand on my
shoulder. "Keep your chin up, Troy."

Then the man from the Youth Development Council said it was
time to go. I wiped the tears from my face and hugged Mom and
Dad hard one more time. I didn't want to let go. Finally, I grabbed
my little blue suitcase and walked with the man in the suit. As we
got close to the exit, I turned and waved one more time.

Mill Valley was nothing like Children's Center or the Brantfield
Mental Health Institute. Those places were for kids that had mental
illnesses. Mill Valley mostly held kids that were considered juvenile delinquents, waiting to go to court for their alleged offenses or
being evaluated to decide in which facility they belonged. Maybe
some of them had mental illnesses, but a lot of these kids already

knew what it was like being a younger version of an inmate in a prison. They were hardened to the experience, lacking the emotional attachments that most kids their age had, or at least showing that they cared about anyone else.

Mill Valley was limbo. Some kids were waiting to go on trial. Other kids were waiting for a room to open up in a state facility where they would serve their time and try to get back on the right track.

When I arrived at the Mill Valley Detention Center, one of the counselors took my blue suitcase. He said he would keep it until it was time for me to go someplace else. I wanted to hug my stuffed animal, but I didn't get to keep it with me. The counselor led me into the section of the building for the younger kids. It was loud. Kids were laughing and yelling. Some kids were in constant motion, pushing and grabbing other kids. A few kids were just sitting on the floor. The counselor brought me through the main common room. I was hoping I could find a corner to hide in. One of the boys yelled to me, loud enough so all the other kids could hear him.

"Hey, do you want a handy?" he asked.

All the kids laughed and then stared at me, waiting for my response. My face flushed with embarrassment.

"What?" I asked meekly.

"Do you want a handy?" he repeated.

The suspense built as he waited for my answer. I didn't know what he meant, but I felt like I had to say something.

"I guess so," I agreed.

"He wants a handy," he yelled to everyone, but no one in particular. I felt the scorn of the room, as they laughed louder than before.

"Shut up," yelled the counselor to the troublemaker.

I wasn't sure why everyone laughed at me, but I felt stupid. I found out later he had asked me if I wanted a hand job. He had jokingly propositioned me sexually. I was seven years old and was now part of world that I didn't even know existed.

The counselor took me to my room. He glanced in through the small, wire-meshed window. He opened the big door and showed me my black, iron bed with a skinny mattress and pillow. He then got me my institution clothes and told me to change into them. Then he brought me back out to the noisy Day Room, as it was called, with the other kids. The counselor told the kid who made me the brunt of his joke to leave me alone. I stood by myself, self conscious and lonely.

These kids were not like Robin and Brian, and certainly not like my younger brother, Doug. I never liked staying at Children's Center or Brantfield, but the kids weren't mean. It was different at Mill Valley. These kids were tough and street smart. They didn't seem afraid of anyone. They listened to the counselors when they had to, but as soon as the counselors were out of view, they did what they wanted to do.

I had to meet with Dr. Hallett, a psychiatrist, who asked me a lot of questions. I didn't mind, because it got me away from the other kids. I told the psychiatrist about my long history, about the things that happened in the middle of the night, about not remembering doing these things. All the usual stuff that rambled automatically from my mouth.

During the day, I kept to myself and stayed out of the way of the bigger kids, especially the ones who got into fights. I wrote letters and drew pictures and sent them home. I really looked forward to the letters and post cards I got in return.

* * * *

Dear Troy,

This card should bring back happy memories.

Twisting and everything. I'm in a happy mood, because it is Wednesday and in a little while Dad and I will be seeing you. We got your letter today. I think it's the nicest one you ever wrote. Thank you and know something? I miss you, too—very much.

Lots and lots of love

Mom

* * * *

The picture on the post card was of Stockford Beach. Sometimes, the whole family went there, only a few miles away from our home in Belport. Stockford Beach was like a carnival with lots of rides and a big, wooden roller coaster. The post card reminded me of dancing the twist, like Chubby Checkers, to the loud rock and roll music playing from one of the rides. I liked showing off sometimes, and I twisted and turned to the beat of the music like a street performer while people walked by and smiled at me.

* * * *

Hi Troy,

Here is a picture for you to draw and paint. I sure did enjoy seeing you Wednesday night. Your muscles are getting so hard, just like your head. I bet you would like to punch me for saying that. Will see you soon.

love

Dad

* * * *

Dad always joked and made me laugh. In another post card, Dad wrote to tell me that he was going to work at a different store, this one called the Daily Cruller. He didn't have to go to work until 10 in the morning. I sure would have felt better if Dad had been home at night and in the morning when Mom came in to wake me up for school.

* * * *

Dear Troy,

Edith is in the hospital and the neighbors are taking turns caring for Edith's kids. Brian got picked to pitch on the Little League Giants. The kids liked the pictures you made. Brian wishes he was old enough to visit you. I talked to Aunty Rosa on the phone and she said to be sure and tell you she was asking for you. Are you making more paintings? I'm making a picture for you. Sure miss you.

Lots of love

Mom

* * * *

I felt bad that Edith was in the hospital. I missed Edith too. I wished I could have watched Brian pitch. He was a lefty and could throw hard. I wanted to play Little League ball when I got older and was back home.

* * * *

At night, I felt sad and sometimes cried. One night, I woke up in a panic. I had dreamt that some guy was trying to catch me. It was dark out and rainy. I couldn't see him, but I felt like he was near me. Suddenly, he grabbed me from behind. I tried to scream, but he covered my mouth. I couldn't breathe. He blocked my screams so nobody could hear me. I kept trying to yell, but all I could do was make a muffled sound. I struggled to breathe and get away. I tried to yell. ... . Then I woke up.

I felt panicked. My heart was pounding and I tried to catch my breath. I looked around my dark room. I realized it was a dream, but I was shaken. I clutched my pillow, and made sure I kept my eyes open and stayed awake. I hated that feeling. Being afraid ... yelling but nobody hearing me ... not being able to breathe. I was afraid I would have to go through it again if I fell back asleep. I stayed in bed in the dark with my eyes wide open until it was time for breakfast.

There were a few bigger kids that were kind of the bosses of everyone, or at least it seemed like that. I tried to stay out of their way, and not talk to them unless they said something to me. It seemed like all the other kids were bigger than me, but I was able to avoid getting picked on. Sometimes, kids would start pushing each other or fight. But kids were transferred to other places a lot so things kept changing.

Probably to get some of that pent-up energy out, the counselors sometimes let kids box with real boxing gloves. Everyone would yell when one of the kids got hit hard or knocked down. I liked to watch it, but I sure didn't want to fight anyone.

* * * *

Dear mom,

How are you and dad? Are you coming to see me this week? You can only come on Weds. How are Robin, Brian and Doug. Friday night some of *the children boxed. I watched them box. I will be looking forward to Weds. I can do a flip now.*

Your love

Troy

* * * *

The counselors had a small office with windows off of the Day Room. Sometimes they stayed in there, but usually at night time more than during the day. One Friday night, one of the counselors came into my room after lights out and bedtime for everyone.

"Do you like boxing?" he asked.

"Ya," I said quietly.

"How would you like to watch some of the Friday Night boxing on TV?" he asked.

"Sure," I said.

"Well, come with me."

He took me to their office. There I sat with the counselors and watched the boxing matches with them. When I got tired, one of the counselors took me back to my room. As far as I knew, I was the only kid they ever asked to join them. I looked forward to Friday nights the rest of my time there.

In the middle of April, Dr. Hallett reported his findings of his evaluation of me to the court, where, according to Mom, he suggested that I needed psychiatric help.

I was supposed to go to court to find out where I would go next.

Mom mailed me a card with a picture of three little innocent girls, maybe angels, standing in a snow-covered field, playing musical instruments.

* * * *

Dear Troy,

Ran out of postcards, so I thought you might like this little picture almost as well. Didn't find out 'til tonite that the hearing at court tomorrow A.M. had been postponed 'til next week. In a way I was disappointed because I was looking forward to seeing you in the morning. But now will be able to see you Wed. nite and that's good, huh?

Did you ever get your crackerjacks? Hope so. See you Wed. night. Lots and lots of love

Mom

* * * *

The following week, the judge officially transferred custody of me to the Youth Development Council. He comforted Mom and Dad, saying that they had done the right thing. In about a week or two, he said I would be sent from the Mill Valley Detention Center to another facility to begin treatment. With the Youth Development Council now in charge of my care, they would decide where I would go next.

9
Whitford Training Center

As the United States moved more towards industry in the 18th and 19th centuries, there was a shift in population and life style, with the informal network of small town America dissipating. Along with the transition to city life came increased juvenile poverty, truancy and crime. With limited options, the courts sent troubled youth to the same prisons that housed adult criminals, with disastrous results. In New York, Thomas Eddy and John Griscom helped form the Society for the Prevention of Pauperism, intended to keep juveniles out of prisons. They pushed for new facilities designed specifically for children and adolescents. In 1825, the New York House of Refuge was established and became an alternative for scuffling youth. It quickly became a model for similar institutions that sprang up across the country.

* * * *

Youth Development Council

May 20, 1964

Dear Mr. and Mrs. Kane,

The Youth Development Council has had your boy, Troy, under study at our Reception Center. Careful consideration of the factors involved in this case has led us to decide that the boy's best interest would be served by placing him for a period of training at the Whitford Training Center, at Whitford.

He was placed in the Whitford Training Center on May 20, 1964. You will hear from the Superintendent of that school regarding visiting days, etc., and please address any further communications regarding your boy to that school from this date on.

Sincerely yours,

Burt Ferguson

Superintendent

* * * *

May 20, 1964

Dear Mrs. Kane;

Your son Troy Kane was admitted to the Whitford Training Center, Residential Treatment Unit on Wednesday, May 20, 1964. Whitford Training Center is located on Route 57 on Pine St., Whitford.

You may visit your son on the second and last Sunday of each month from two to four o'clock in the afternoon.

Very truly yours,

Luis Schneider

Assistant Superintendent

* * * *

It was a 50-mile drive from Mill Valley to the Whitford Training Center in Whitford, a small town outside of Hanville. There were large trees everywhere, and as we got closer, we drove by a big lake. It was a lot bigger than Lake Cramby where we used to go swimming when we lived in Powell. It turned out to be the Hickory Reservoir, used by all the towns in the area for their drinking water. The front entrance to the Whitford Training Center featured a semi-circle wall on each side of the driveway that looked like it had been chiseled out of the hillside. A tall pillar of cement defined the boundary of each wall, topped with a round cement ball like a cherry on an ice cream sundae. Similar to a southern estate, flowering trees lined the long drive up to the main buildings.

Whitford Training Center sat up on a hill at the end of the drive, its red-brick buildings snugly fit into the wooded, hilly land, as if nature had decided this was a good place for kids to try to get their lives in order. Connected to the older part of the building, there was a new, two-story rectangular structure that looked like a college dorm, except for the metal grates that covered the windows.

Metal grates on the windows to prevent escape

In the back and far side of the property were three tiers, look-ing like flattened steps cut out of the hilly land. The top shelf was the smallest, and had a dirt basketball court on it. The middle area was the largest, with a backstop and baseball diamond on one end stretching to the single set of monkey bars positioned all the way at the other end. None of the kids had the power to hit a ball all the way to the monkey bars from the baseball diamond. But Mr. Kirk, the activities counselor, hit long, arching fly balls over the monkey bars almost every time he got up. From the middle level, the hill graded down to the lowest plane, flattened out briefly and then sloped downward towards Route 57 and the reservoir. Covered by the frequent snow storms in the winter, this hill was a favorite place for sledding. On the outskirts of this level was a cluster of apple trees. You weren't supposed to go to the apple orchard, because that put you too close to the property line and possible escape.

The Training Center was for boys only, with separate wards for the teenage boys and the younger kids. This was not a mental institution; it was a place where you learned to behave yourself. The counselors weren't there to reason with you. When they told you to do something, you had better do it.

I arrived on a warm, sunny afternoon and met Mr. Cranwell, the Superintendent. He sat me down in his office and told me that Whitford Training Center was a training school for boys. This place gave boys, who for one reason or another had difficulty staying out of trouble, another shot.

"Keep your nose clean and listen to the counselors, and you will get along fine here," he advised me.

The first day went by pretty fast. I got some clothes, got settled in my room and went out on the playground area with the other kids. I had supper in a large dining hall. The food was okay. After supper, we watched TV and then went to bed.

I was happy to go to bed because I was tired from the busy day, but when I put my head on the pillow, an empty feeling overcame me. I wanted to go home. I missed Mom. I missed Dad. I missed Robin and Brian and Doug. I missed wearing my own clothes and having my own things. Why did I have to go away? What was wrong with me? As I exhaled, tears formed in the corners of my eyes and a muffled cry escaped from deep within me. I tried hard not to let anyone hear me crying. Without any answers to my questions, I drifted off to sleep.

"Up and at 'em, move and strip 'em," bellowed someone down the far end of the hall to start my second day at Whitford Training Center.

"Let's go, move it," he said as the loud voice got closer.

I jumped out of bed, and stood not knowing what to do. A man with short, red hair popped his head into my room.

"You must be the new kid. I'm Mr. Sullivan. What's your name?" he asked.

"Um ... Troy," I muttered.

"Don't be shy. Speak up when I talk to you. Strip the sheets and pillow case off your bed and put them out in the hallway," he barked.

He quickly made his way back down the hall.

"I won't tell you again. Up and at 'em, move and strip 'em," he yelled as he poked his head into each room in the long hallway.

Whack!

"No, Mr. Sullivan, I'll get up," a boy cried out.

I peeked out my door. Mr. Sullivan must have slapped one of the kids who was slow getting up. Mr. Sullivan's forearm muscles popped out underneath the curly, red hair blanketing his arms. Just about all the kids were now standing outside their rooms, tucking in their shirts and tying the laces on their sneakers. Suddenly, I noticed that I was the only kid still in pajamas. Now Mr. Sullivan was making his way back towards our end of the hallway. I wondered if I should sneak back into my room and get changed, but I didn't know if I would get in trouble for leaving the line. I was too scared to ask him anything, so I just stood there in my pajamas. It didn't take long for him to notice.

"Troy, you're supposed to get dressed so you can come to breakfast," he said.

"Oh. I'm sorry. Um ... I was .... umm," I stammered.

"Well, hurry up. We don't have all morning," Mr. Sullivan interjected.

"Yes, sir," I said and hurried into my room to change.

My practice of dressing and undressing quickly to the 1812

Overture came in handy, although I didn't dare hum any songs. I quickly got ready, grabbing a pair of plaid shorts and a striped, short-sleeve shirt. My mismatched clothes selection fit right in with the rest of the kids.

I didn't know anyone at breakfast, so I just sat at the table and didn't say anything. After breakfast, Mr. Sullivan got us organized and off we went to school, which was a classroom down the hall. I found out there were only a few weeks left before the summer break. We had to do a little reading and we got to write a letter home. The teacher checked our letters. He did some teaching, but mostly made sure no one was fooling around. I kept quiet and made sure I didn't get in any trouble.

In the afternoon, we went out. We could play on either the middle or top level. I drifted towards the far end of the baseball diamond, to the monkey bars. There were a few of us climbing, and swinging back and forth on the metal rungs. Each of us fluidly moved without interfering with the others. I recognized one of the kids from Mr. Sullivan's morning inspection.

For supper, we had spaghetti and meatballs. I liked Mom's better, but it was still good. I found out that some nights after dinner, there was a big softball game with the kids and counselors on each team. Tonight we were going to play.

After supper, we went out to the softball diamond. Mr Kirk assigned each kid to one of the teams. I was hoping I'd be on his team, but he put me on the other team.

"I'm up first," yelled the boy I recognized from the morning inspection and monkey bars.

Mr. Johnson was one of the counselors on our team. He was a tall man with dark hair combed straight back.

"Rocco, if I bat you first, can I count on you to get on base?" he asked with a broad smile revealing a gold tooth.

"Of course," Rocco shot right back at him.

"That's what I like to hear," he responded.

"Okay, everyone come over to the bench." I wanted to jump up and down, and raise my hand. "Pick me, Mr. Johnson, pick me ... I'll get a hit." But I was too scared to say anything as Mr. Johnson called out the batting order. Then he stopped.

"Whoa, wait a minute, who's this?" Mr. Johnson asked as he saw me standing towards the back of the group.

The kids turned their heads to see who he was talking about. "I'm Troy," I said quietly.

"Well, nice to meet you Troy."

He finished putting the batting order in place. Mr. Kirk took the mound to pitch for the other team. The counselors always pitched, because the kids couldn't throw the ball over the plate.

"Okay, Rocco, let's see what you got," Mr. Kirk said to Rocco as he got ready to throw the first pitch.

Rocco dug his back foot deep into the batter's box. He smacked the tip of the bat on the plate several times and stared back confidently at Mr. Kirk. The first pitch floated slowly in the air. Rocco swung as hard as he could, almost falling down, and missed the ball.

"Strike one," said Mr. Kirk.

"Rocco, don't try to kill it," advised Mr. Johnson.

"C'mon, Rocco. You can do it," came from our bench.

The next pitch Rocco swung just as hard, but this time hit it pretty good. It rolled hard right over third base and into the outfield. Rocco threw the bat in the air, almost hitting the catcher, and started running to first. As he raised each arm up like a sprinter does in the 100-yard dash, like clockwork, he turned his head all the way to one side and then to the other, perfectly synchronizing his upward-swinging arm movements with his side-to-side head twists. With all that motion and energy, he seemed to move faster than he actually did. I wondered if he got dizzy running like that.

The outfielder on the other team fielded the ball and threw it in towards second base. Rocco didn't care. He wasn't stopping at first base. His arms were flailing and his head twisting and churning faster and faster. But the ball reached second base way before Rocco did, and he was out by a mile.

"You're out," called Mr. Kirk.

"No way," reacted Rocco. "I was safe."

"Rocco, let's go. You were out," said Mr. Johnson.

Rocco kicked at the dirt as he came off the field. Dad always taught us to be good sports. If I did that at home, Dad would have made me sit down and cool off. We got another hit in the inning, but we didn't score any runs.

As the other team came off the field, they handed their baseball gloves to the kids on our team. I walked slowly to the field hoping someone would give me a glove, but no one did. Mr. Kirk noticed me standing there, and he threw me a glove. Mr. Johnson told me to come stand in the outfield near him.

The first kid got out. Then Mr. Johnson started to hum and then sing in a deep voice.

He was really singing! I looked around at the other kids. I figured everyone would be laughing, or at least making faces about the counselor singing during the game. But nobody did anything.

The second batter reached first base when the ball went right between our second basemen's legs into the outfield. I ran to get the ball, but there were a lot of kids in the outfield and another kid beat me to it. The next batter hit a line drive to left field for another hit.

Mr. Johnson didn't seem worried at all about the other team getting a few runners on base. He kept on piping out the song, Moon River.

Our team made a few errors and then it was Mr. Kirk's turn to bat. Suddenly, a lot of the kids in the field turned and ran towards the monkey bars at the far end of the field. I had no idea what was happening.

Mr. Johnson said, "Troy, you better get out there by the monkey bars and see if you can catch Mr. Kirk's long hit, cause no one else can."

"Okay," I said as I ran out to the monkey bars.

Mr. Johnson stayed right where he was. Most of our team was now standing around the monkey bars. Something big was going to happen. I just didn't think anyone could hit the ball that far. The first pitch was a little low and Mr. Kirk didn't swing at it. But the next pitch, he launched high into the air. The ball seemed to defy gravity, as it soared higher and higher, momentarily joining the white puffy clouds above. The kids started running towards it. Some ran in and some ran out. I ran to my right and in a little. A lot of the kids started calling for it.

"I got it, I got it!"

"No, it's mine."

"Get out of the way. I got it!"

It looked like it was coming right to me, but then it went way over my head and rolled past the monkey bars into the deep grass. We all rushed to find it. By the time one of the kids found the ball and threw it towards the infield, Mr. Kirk had trotted around the bases and crossed home plate.

What a hit! I figured he must be good enough to play in the major leagues.

They didn't score any more runs that inning, and it was our ups. When it was my turn to hit, we had a runner on second base. I stepped into the batter's box. I held my bat slightly above my shoulders and my hands back just like Dad had taught me. I took a few practice swings, trying to keep my swing level.

"Oh, we've got a lefty here," called out Mr. Kirk.

His first pitch was a little high and I didn't swing. Dad always said I didn't swing at bad pitches. Mr. Kirk's next offering was belt high and I took a good swing at it. I hit a slow grounder between the shortstop and third base. The throw to first bounced in the dirt and got away from the first baseman. As it rolled past him, I rounded first and took off towards second. I slid into second just beating the throw.

My heart was pounding. Mr. Kirk said, "Watch out for the new kid. He's fast."

I felt a little smile come across my lips. The next batter popped out to end the inning. I wished Dad had been there to see me get a hit and run the bases.

The first mail I got was a post card from Mrs. Jordan, the psychologist from the Roosevelt School. She said Mom had called her to tell her I was there. The next day, I got a post card from Mom, with a picture of Belport Beach on the front.

* * * *

May 25, 1964

Dear Troy,

So you are at a new address and we didn't even know it til you had left. The place you are staying at is the one Mrs. Jordan has visited and says is such a wonderful place. I hope you will like it there as much as she says you will. I miss you very much. Especially since we didn't see you last Sunday. See you on visiting day.

Love

Mom

* * * *

Towards the end of my stay at Mill Valley, Mom got a job at Slater County Medical Center in the Central Supply Room. She called it CSR. She had to clean up things they used to take care of the patients, like metal bowls and other things they could use again. She also had to put together the supplies the doctors used to operate on people and supplies the nurses needed every day to take care of patients. Everything had to be sterile, so Mom had to wear hospital gowns just like a doctor or nurse did. It was hard work, but Mom said she liked working in a hospital.

Mom had always been interested in medicine. When she and Dad were going to get married, Grampa had given her a choice of paying for her wedding reception or paying for her education to become a nurse. She chose the beautiful wedding day. She might have still tried to become a nurse, but she was pregnant soon after getting married and she didn't have time to take care of all of us and go to college. It was probably too much money for Mom and Dad anyway.

Mom's boss in CSR was Mr. Wilton. She didn't like him. He treated everyone like they weren't as good as him. Sometimes he'd yell at them if something wasn't just like he said it was supposed to be. Mom made friends with one of the people she worked with, a young black woman named Vicki. She had beauty, spirit and a knack for telling a good story. Vicki had a boyfriend named Eddie, who was smaller than she was. Little Eddie she called him. But Little Eddie couldn't be trusted. He was always up to no good, like getting drunk or chasing other women, but it always sounded funny when Vicki relayed her tales. Mom couldn't understand why Vicki didn't just get rid of him. She said Vicki could do a lot better than Little Eddie.

Mom worked from 2:30 in the afternoon until 11 at night. Dad drove her to work each afternoon. It was less than 10 miles from Belport to Slater County Medical Center in Mason Heights. If there wasn't a lot of traffic, like when Dad picked up Mom after work, it would only take about half an hour. But afternoon traffic going into

Mason Heights was always bad. Dad hated driving over the Bowen Bridge leading to Mason Heights, with a bunch of lanes of bumper-to-bumper traffic inching through toll booths and then funneling back into three lanes. Cars jockeyed back and forth, darting forward one or two feet at a time, then jamming on their breaks to avoid hitting the car in front or beside them. It was a game of chicken, which was counter to Dad's gentler personality. Who could get in better position? Who would back down?

"What a winner," Dad would say sarcastically when someone cut him off. Despite hating the traffic, Dad always gave Mom a ride. That left Robin, the oldest kid, in charge of Brian and Doug. Brian didn't like this at all, and it caused a lot of friction between Robin and Brian. Now 12 years old, Robin was also responsible for making supper.

* * * *

Picture of Sailing Boat at Belport Beach
May 1964
Whitford Training Center

Dear Troy,

How do you like where you are? We haven't had the car for three days as Dad is getting everything fixed on it so it will be in good condition for us to come and see you, Sun May 31. I was supposed to work that day but I swapped weekends with another girl so I can be off to see you. It's been so long! Won't we have a lot to tell each other. We miss you very much and just can't wait to see you.

Lots of love

Mom

* * * *

One afternoon, before we went outside to play, Mr. Sullivan told us to line up. He took us to a room where they did all the laundry. It had big washing machines and dryers. As we walked into the room, there was an enormous pile of clothes on the floor in the middle of the room. I figured these were everyone's dirty clothes and we were going to have to wash them.

"All right. You know the drill. Pick out your clothes. No pushing or you won't get anything," he warned.

Immediately, kids reached into the pile of clothes, which were clean, and pulled out shirts and shorts and socks and underwear. Somehow they seemed to know what they wanted to wear, and grabbed these items before someone else did. I caught on quickly. I reached into the pile, grabbed out a pair of blue shorts and held them up to my waist. They looked like they would fit so I kept them. I grabbed some white socks. They didn't match exactly, but they didn't have any holes in them. I pulled out a striped shirt, but it was way too big. Then, I saw a white polo shirt. I measured it against myself, and it looked like it fit. It had a red crest on the left side of the chest. I really liked it. I tucked it under the clothes I had picked out so nobody would try to take it. I picked out my other stuff. When we finished, my wardrobe was made up of a strange collection of clothes that didn't match, and were more often than not, a little big for my small frame.

"Okay, go back to your rooms and put your clothes away. I don't want to see any of these clothes out on your bed or dresser. I'll be checking so put them away, and make it fast," he barked.

When I got to my room, I put my clothes in the dresser right away so Mr. Sullivan wouldn't get mad at me. However, I quickly changed my shirt and put on the white polo shirt and tucked it into my shorts.

* * * *

May 26, 1964

Dear Mom and Dad,

We go out every day and I play on the monkey bars. We go to school. How are Robin, Brian and Doug? Did you help Doug with the letter yet? Well if you didn't I hope you will. Dad did you start playing baseball yet? I hope you did. How is Edith? I love her. Give her a big kiss for me. I know some of the names of my books and here is the name of my book "Town and Country." Well that is all I have to say goodbye. oh next Sunday is visiting Sunday.

Your loving son,

Troy Kane

* * * *

The next day began like the others. "Up and at "em, move and strip em," hollered Mr. Sullivan. I jumped out of bed, and quickly pulled the sheet off my bed and put it out in the hallway. I got dressed, and slipped my white polo shirt back on. I was standing outside of my room ready for inspection in no time, as Mr. Sullivan worked his way up and down the hallway checking each room.

We had to read aloud from our Town and Country book during school. I felt a little nervous because I didn't know anybody, but I guess I did okay. Nobody made fun of me or seemed to care I was reading. There were a few kids that couldn't read much at all. In the afternoon, Mr. Kirk told us about the Memorial Day field competition on Saturday. He said there would be all kinds of races, and field events, like the softball throw. The winners would get ribbons.

I woke up early on Saturday, before Mr. Sullivan or one of the other counselors yelled to get the day in motion. It was quiet, as the sun peeked through the grated bars on my window, forming little rectangles on my bed and floor. My window looked out towards the reservoir. There were some bushes and flowers lining the wall of the building. I saw something small fluttering in front of the window. It was a miniature bird. Like a helicopter suspended in the air, it floated slightly above the flower, nourished itself and then darted to another bright red flower. It was a beautiful little hummingbird. I had never seen one before, and I couldn't take my eyes off it. Then it decided it was time to go somewhere else in search of more nectar.

I was already dressed for the day when the counselors began to wake everyone up. I wished I could have worn my white polo shirt, but they wouldn't let you wear the same shirt each day. I had to put it back into the laundry.

After breakfast, we made our way outside to begin the competition. I couldn't stop thinking about winning a ribbon. I was nervous, but I hoped I was good enough to beat some of the other kids. Mr. Kirk met us in front of the shed where he kept all the sports equipment.

"Okay, today is the Memorial Day Track and Field Day. There are a lot of different races and events," he said.

And he held up the ribbons we could win. Like all the other kids, my eyes were glued to those silky ribbons, which were purple with a yellow, braided string dangling from the top. On it read, *Memorial Day Events*. Boy, I really wanted to win one.

"Good sportsmanship is just as important as running fast or jumping high. If you don't show good sportsmanship, you won't get any ribbons," he said.

It was a sunny day and hot already. I was in one event called the Duck Walk. You had to squat down, bend your knees and walk on the balls of your feet as fast as you could. It made you look kind of silly, I guess like a duck. It was hard to go fast. I didn't win, but I did pretty good. The next day though, my thighs were killing me.

I ran in the 100-yard Dash. There were a lot of kids, so they split us up into a bunch of smaller groups. Mr. Kirk called them heats. Rocco was in the heat before me. He twisted his head side-to-side, and moved his arms up and down at a fierce pace. He looked like he would beat everyone, but when the race was over, he ended up finishing towards the back. Boy was he mad.

Then I ran my 100-yard Dash. I didn't win my heat, but I did well.

After we finished all the events, Mr. Kirk and the other counselors handed out the ribbons. I got one!

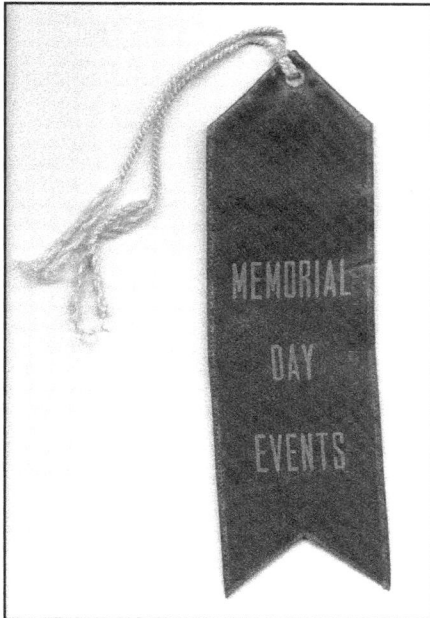

My prized Memorial Day Ribbon

135

On the back, Mr. Kirk had written my name and the 100 yard dash event.

The next day was Visiting Day. It was sunny and warm again. My whole family came. There were other families there to see their kids, but I thought there would be a lot more. Maybe some of the other families had car problems. Before we could visit, Mr. Cranwell, the man in charge of Whitford Training Center, called all the kids together.

"Now today your families have come a long way to see you. This is going to be a fun day. I want to see smiles on your faces. Show them that you are happy. You *will* have fun," he ordered.

Finally, Mr. Cranwell set us free to visit. I came over to see my family. It had been two and a half months since I had seen Robin, Brian or Doug. We were kind of quiet at first. Then, Mom broke the silence.

"What's that in your hand?"

"Look I won a ribbon yesterday!" I said and proudly held out my ribbon.

"Let me see that," said Dad. "That is a beauty. Wow, the 100-yard Dash."

Everyone was impressed. I felt so proud.

"Well, I brought a picnic lunch. We have ham sandwiches and chips and chocolate chip cookies, and some nice cold, apple juice to drink," Mom said.

Dad spread out the blanket on the grass, and we staked out our temporary family homestead. After lunch, Brian said, "Do you want to play Run the Bases?"

"Sure," I said.

"What can we use for bases?" asked Doug.

Mom gave us a few paper plates. Mom and Dad were the catchers and all of us kids were the runners. Dad threw the ball to Mom but she missed it and we all ran. Brian and I ran to Dad's base and back to Mom's base and didn't get caught. Mom threw the ball to Dad, and Robin took off. Doug started running late, and it looked like Dad would tag him, but he swiped his hand right by Doug. We all laughed. After a few minutes, Mom went to sit on the blanket. Brian was the new catcher. Dad faked throwing the ball and we all started running towards him. Doug didn't realize Dad had the ball in his hand the whole time, but he still reached his base. I think Dad let him be safe.

"Anyone want something to drink or eat?" Mom asked.

It was great to be able to have a snack whenever I felt like it.

"Sure," I said.

We sat on the blanket for a few minutes while we ate and drank.

"What do you do during the day?" Mom asked.

"I go to school in the morning. There are eight kids in my class, but two are going home soon," I said. "We get to play outside in the afternoon and one night we played baseball and I got a hit. And Mr. Kirk hit a home run over the monkey bars!"

After a few more minutes, Robin asked, "Anyone want to play hide and seek?"

Robin counted first. There weren't a lot of good places to hide, but it was still fun. But before long, the two hours were up. I felt an aching feeling in my stomach. Dad folded the blanket and Mom got everything together. It was time for them to go, and time for me to stay.

It didn't seem fair, but I didn't say anything. I just felt sad. We hugged one last time, while tears streamed down my cheeks. Then my family left, down the winding driveway to Route 57 and on their way on the long drive back to Belport, and I was back in training school as a juvenile delinquent.

I didn't know anything about it, but before the visiting hours, Mom and Dad met with Mr. Cranwell. He did this for parents of new kids to let them know what Whitford Training Center was all about and answer any questions they had. Mom wanted to find out about the therapy I was getting. Mr. Cranwell explained that Whitford Training Center taught kids how to act, by giving them a stable environment and requiring them to show respect to the counselors and other kids. As part of the initial evaluation, I would meet with a psychiatrist within the first few weeks. Then before I left Whitford Training Center to go home, they would do another psychological evaluation of me, but those were the only times I would see a psychiatrist.

This was not what Mom and Dad expected. They had given up custody of me so that they could get me the treatment I needed. Apparently, the State had ignored Dr. Hallett's evaluation of me and treatment recommendations from the Mill Valley Detention Center. Mrs. Jordan had given this place such a high recommendation. Now, my parents didn't have custody of me, and I was in a training school, basically a detention center for juvenile delinquents.

* * * *

Picture of Museum of Science
June 1, 1964
Whitford Training Center

Dear Troy,

I enjoyed so much seeing you Sunday. Next time we come I'll bring a picnic lunch. I'm so proud of the ribbon you won. I'm going to mail you a little package tomorrow. I'm working this Sat and Sun so I can have off to see you the week after.

Lots of love

Mom

* * * *

One morning, Mr. Sullivan told me I had to go to Mr. Cranwell's office. It felt like I had to see the principal at the Roosevelt School. As I walked down the hall towards his office, I tried to figure out what I did wrong? What if they said I got up in the middle of the night and wrecked something?

As I nervously approached his office, Mr. Cranwell was coming out of it.

"Oh, come inside Troy. I'd like you to meet someone," he said. "This is Dr. Gifford. He is a psychiatrist. When our kids first come here, Dr. Gifford talks to them so he can help us understand them better. He is going to talk to you this morning."

Dr. Gifford said, "Nice to meet you, Troy. Let's go across the hall to that office."

I nodded and mumbled that I was glad to meet him too. When we sat down, Dr. Gifford asked me a lot of questions.

We talked about the things I got in trouble for at home. How I used razor blades to cut Mom's and Robin's legs and feet during the night when they were sleeping. How I was jealous of my brothers. He wrote notes as I talked. It seemed like we talked for a long time. He was nice, but I was glad I wouldn't have to see him every week.

Mom sent me a lot of packages and post cards and letters. I got something most days. I really looked forward to it. Sometimes at night before I went to bed, I read my post cards and letters over again. One of the things I got from Mom was a little booklet that showed how Indians lived, and the sign language they used. We got to watch a movie that had cowboys and Indians fighting. The Indian chief was named Cochise. He was big and strong and didn't let anyone beat him up or take his land. I liked some of the cowboys, but when we played cowboys and Indians, I always said I was Cochise. I tried to make the signs and run fast like he did. One afternoon, I took my Indian booklet out of my top drawer, where I kept my post cards and ribbon, and showed Rocco. He liked it a lot, too.

After playing the next afternoon, we went back to our rooms before we went to the dining hall for supper. We had a little time, so I decided to look at my Indian book. I reached into my drawer to get it, but it wasn't there. Did I forget to put it away earlier? I looked around the room. Maybe it fell behind my bed. Nope. I looked everywhere, but I couldn't find it. Where was it?

At dinner, I told Rocco I couldn't find it anywhere. He said maybe I put it somewhere else or let another kid borrow it and forgot. I knew I didn't do that. I loved to read about the Indians. There was no way I would let someone else borrow it, and forget I did. After supper, I looked again in my drawer. I noticed that my Indian booklet wasn't the only thing that was missing. There were also empty rectangles where someone had torn off the stamps from some of my post cards. Someone had stolen my stamps that I used to send letters home. And worst of all, my Memorial Day ribbon was gone!

Suddenly, it hit me that someone had stolen some of my favorite things. I ran out of my room and saw Mr. Johnson walking down the hall checking on us.

"Mr. Johnson, someone stole my Memorial Day ribbon and Indian book!" I said.

"Are you sure you didn't put 'em somewhere and forgot where?" he asked.

"No. I put all my stuff in my top drawer, I'll show ya," I answered.

He came into my room and I opened my drawer. I showed him the torn post cards and told him again that I kept everything in my top drawer. I was almost crying.

"Okay, okay. Take it easy. I'll take a look around and see if I can find them," he said.

He started checking the other kids' rooms. He went to Rocco's room, which was a few doors down from mine.

"Rocco, I want to take a look around your room," he said.

"What for?" Rocco fired back.

"I'm just checking," Mr. Johnson said.

Mr. Johnson pulled open his dresser drawers, and there were a bunch of loose cardboard rectangles with stamps glued to them. The Indian booklet was there. There were a few Memorial Day ribbons also. Mr. Johnson checked the back of the ribbons where Mr. Kirk wrote the event we were in and our name on a light piece of cardboard. One ribbon had the cardboard torn off the back.

"Where did you get this stuff?" Mr. Johnson asked while holding up the ribbon and Indian booklet.

"It's mine," Rocco shot back loudly.

"Don't lie to me," said Mr. Johnson as he walked closer to Rocco. "Come with me," Mr. Johnson said in a stern voice.

Mr. Johnson took Rocco down the hall. He was in big trouble. I couldn't believe Rocco stole my favorite things from me. How could he? I had told him about what happened, and he lied right to my face. I thought he was my friend.

* * * *

Picture of Old State House
June 1964
Whitford Training Center

Dear Troy,

How would you like to slide down this banister?
Did you notice the Kennedy stamp? I enjoyed visiting with you Sunday—I've missed seeing and

talking with you. How is school? Brian was on TV on the Kids Clubhouse show. He went with the Cub Scouts. I'll be looking forward to your letter.

Lots of love

Mom

* * * *

I wished I could have watched Brian on TV, but we only got to watch TV at night sometimes. The Cub Scouts sounded like fun.

Mom sent me more post cards keeping me up with what was going on with the family. She was going to work the next weekend so she could come on Visiting Day. She said she would bring me new sneakers, because mine were kind of worn out. Mom and Dad sent me toys and brought some on Visiting Day. I didn't get this much stuff when I lived at home. I think they felt bad that I had to stay there.

Mom said that she got to watch an operation in the hospital. I was glad that I didn't have to see the blood and someone's guts. She also said she saw her therapist, Dr. Harlan, for the last time. She liked him and said he helped her a lot. That is what Mom said she wanted for me, to have a therapist that could help me stop getting in trouble so I could live at home again.

10
A Boy's Dreams

In 1964, Harmon Killebrew was on his way to leading the American League in home runs for the third year in a row. By the standards of the day, at 5"10" and 220 pounds, he was big and strong as an ox. In 22 seasons, he hit 573 home runs. No steroids, no performance-enhancing drugs. He hit tape-measure shots out of the ball park. He was the first player to hit the ball over the left-field roof in Tiger Stadium in Detroit. He hit the longest home run in the history of his home park, Metropolitan Stadium in Minneapolis, some 520 feet in the air.

And yet, for all his strength and accomplishments in baseball, Harmon Killebrew was a quiet and humble man. In a 1963 Sports Illustrated article, when asked about any unusual hobbies he had, he said he liked washing the dishes. Maybe Killebrew was unusual for the time, or maybe the media coverage painted different images of the athletes of the era, but the national past time had a purity that appealed to youngsters across the country. For many kids, there was nothing like watching their heroes play ball, and dreaming that someday they would get a chance to wear a major league uniform.

* * * *

Moon river, wider than a mile
Mmmm, mmmm, mm mm mm mm

I was wearing my new baseball glove that Mom and Dad brought up on Visiting Day. I didn't mind being on Mr. Johnson's team. It gave me the chance to catch one of Mr. Kirk's long fly balls. I had been practicing throwing the ball up as high as I could and trying to chase it down before it hit the ground. I was getting pretty good at it.

When Mr. Kirk came to the plate, the game came to a standstill as we all raced to the monkey bars. Most of the kids stood in front of the monkey bars, but I was happy to stand behind them. There was more room to move around and go after the ball, and sometimes Mr. Kirk hit it that far.

On the first pitch, he clobbered one high and deep to left field. It looked like it was going a little to the left of the monkey bars. I started moving that way. As I took each step, my head bobbed up and down and the ball seemed to dance in the air. It climbed higher and higher in the sky. The kids frantically bumped and caromed off each other and the monkey bars like pinballs bouncing off rubber bumpers in an arcade game.

As gravity began to gain control of the orbital, it shot down from the sky heading to the left of the monkey bars. I ran as hard as I could. I wanted to catch that ball. I was *going to* catch that ball. I put my glove up, waiting to feel the impact of it hitting the web of my glove, but it sailed over my head. That was the closest I had ever come to catching one of Mr. Kirk's hits, but I overran it. There was a mad scramble for the ball. I almost got to it, but one of the bigger kids banged into me and knocked me out of the way. He grabbed the ball and hurled it towards the infield. Mr. Kirk had already touched home plate before the ball got there. Another home run for him. I didn't know how he did it, but I was sure that one day I would snag one of his moon shots.

That night, I replayed the game in my head, fantasizing that I snared one of Mr. Kirk's blasts out by the monkey bars.

"Up and at 'em, move and strip 'em," barked Mr. Sullivan. After breakfast, we went to the laundry room to pick out our clothes for the week from the pile on the floor. Mr. Sullivan gave us the okay, and we started clothes shopping, institution style. The first thing I wanted was my white polo shirt. Well, it wasn't mine, but I really liked that shirt. It made me feel good wearing it. I didn't see it on top so I dug in deeper, pulling clothes up to the surface from the depths of the pile. But I couldn't find it.

"All right, let's go. We don't have all day," warned Mr. Sullivan.

I hadn't picked out anything yet, so I grabbed a few things to keep me going for the week.

"Okay, put your clothes away. Do it right, because I'll be inspecting in a few minutes," he said.

I went to my room and put the clothes away, but I felt a little sad. I wondered who got my white polo shirt.

It wasn't a good day all around for me. At dinner, I noticed one of the other kids wearing the white polo shirt. Lucky stiff, I thought. We had yellow summer squash as part of the menu for dinner. I wasn't paying much attention when I got my food, but I ended up with squash on my plate.

I was a fussy eater, and I knew I wouldn't like it. I wasn't going to try it or like it.

One of the counselors walked by our table and noticed the bright yellow squash, alone and untouched on my plate.

"If you take it, you eat it," he said, pointing at my squash. He stood there with an impatient look on his face.

I stabbed a piece of it with my fork, and brought it up to my nose. It smelled funny so I put it back on my plate.

"We don't waste food here. Eat your squash or I'll help you eat it," he said.

Now I knew I was in trouble. I had to eat it. I put a little piece in my mouth, but I hated it. I knew I wouldn't like it. I spit it out.

"Keep going," he said.

I cut off another piece with my fork and stabbed it. Then I closed my eyes, figuring maybe it wouldn't be so bad if I didn't have to look at it. I was wrong. It was still awful.

Before I spit it out, the counselor said, "Chew it and swallow it." I tried but I couldn't eat it.

"I guess you do need some help," he said and pulled up a chair beside me. "Try it again."

I stalled, cutting up another small piece of squash and pushing it around my plate with my fork. Then I slowly brought the fork and squash back up for another try. This time, the counselor put his hand over my mouth so I couldn't spit it out. It startled me.

"Swallow it," he said in a stern voice as he held me tight so I couldn't get away.

I wanted to spit it out or bite his hand. Tears began to stream down my cheeks. In the excitement, I struggled to breathe through my nose. I swallowed a small piece and almost gagged.

"See, it's not that bad. Squash is good for you. Try another piece," he said.

I wondered to myself, was he crazy? I almost choked. I hated it! What did he mean that it wasn't bad. It was disgusting. When he had put his hand over my mouth, I panicked. Would I be able to breathe? I knew we weren't done yet.

I got another small piece on my fork and put it in my mouth. I paused for a few seconds, as I tried to get my composure back.

"Swallow it," he ordered.

I did and almost vomited. Some of the older kids would have sworn at him, but I didn't say anything. I just wanted it to end.

"Okay, that's good enough this time. Next time, if you take something, you *will* finish it," he warned.

I didn't want to talk to anyone. I just wanted to go to my room and cry into my pillow.

We finished school for the year. It was nice not having to go to school, but that was when we wrote letters home, so I didn't do that as much in the summer. On Visiting Day, I showed Mom and Dad my report card. I got good grades for the few weeks I was in school. I found out I didn't have to stay back and take second grade over again.

* * * *

Picture of Belport Beach and Waves
July 4, 1964
Whitford Training Center

Dear Troy,

Doesn't this water look nice?—but rough. The bathing suit you wanted sent was full of moth holes so I had to buy you one and will mail it tomorrow. I'm sorry it isn't getting to you sooner.

I'm looking forward to seeing you next Sunday. Sure miss getting those nice letters from you. See you soon.

Lots of love

Mom

* * * *

I didn't have a fishing pole, but Mom and Dad got me one and a small tackle box with hooks and plastic things you could use for bait. They got Brian one, too, and he caught a fish off the jetty at Belport beach.

147

I finally got to use my fishing rod and hoped I would catch a fish, just like my older brother did. I wondered how he did it. He would have showed me if I was home. One of the counselors helped me set up the fishing pole and hook with the bait. I put the hook in the water a bunch of times, but I didn't catch anything. One time, my rod bent a little as I reeled in the string, but my hook must have got caught on a rock or some grass in the water. It was kind of boring trying to catch fish. So I put my fishing pole down on the ground and left my hook in the water and walked around.

Then I heard one of the kids call out, "Fish! You got a fish!"

I came running to see who caught a fish. The kid had my fishing pole in his hands. He handed it to me. One of the counselors helped me reel in my fish. I'm not sure what kind it was, but I caught one, with some help. The counselors said they would cook all the fish that we caught. I did not want to eat my fish or any other fish, so I made sure I didn't end up with any on my plate.

There were older kids who stayed in the other part of Whitford Training Center. Sometimes we would see them in the dining room or in another room for school. I heard that some of them had done some awful things to people, and would have gone to jail if they were 18. I found out there was a kid, Pete Holcomb, who was from Belport. Someone said that he stole a car and drove it to Mason Heights before he got caught. I wondered what else he did.

I was afraid that he would want to be friends with me. Then, what would happen if people saw me talking to him when I went back to Belport? What if he told other kids in school where I had been? Would they think I stole cars, too? Would they think I was a juvenile delinquent? I hoped he would stay in Whitford forever, or move really far away from Belport.

Sometimes it seemed like I was going to be stuck at Whitford permanently. Other times, I really could picture myself at home and happy. I wasn't sure why I had to be the one in my family who had to live somewhere else. I didn't know much about being a ward of the state. It didn't seem any different from when I wasn't, but maybe it meant I couldn't go back home. I didn't get in any trouble, so I hoped they would let me go home soon.

My birthday came and went. I was now eight years old. I was hoping my birthday would be on Visiting Day, but it was a Tuesday. At Whitford Training Center, they didn't celebrate birthdays so it was just like any other day. Mom made a birthday cake and brought it on Visiting Day. I got some presents, and it was fun, but it wasn't like a real birthday.

* * * *

Picture of Stage Coach
August 1964
Whitford Training Center

Hi Troy!

I'm sure looking forward to seeing you again. I haven't gone to the beach much lately. We'll be go-ing back to school soon. You'll probably like that. How do you like that stagecoach on the front of this?

Robin

* * * *

It was almost Robin's birthday. She was going to be 13, a teen-ager. Robin was going into the 8th grade in the junior high. If I got released in August, I would be able to go to 3rd grade at the Roosevelt School. There was a Board meeting at the end of the month, where they decided which kids could go home. Maybe I would be on that list.

149

The end of August came and went without any word from the Board about me going home. It was still hot during most days, but at night it cooled off a lot and it got dark a little earlier. We didn't play softball after dinner anymore. I missed Mr. Johnson's deep voice singing Moon River, and getting up to bat with Mr. Kirk warning the other kids about how fast I was, and feeling so good if I got a hit. But the thing I always thought about was trying to catch one of Mr. Kirk's powerful rockets that soared high in the sky and somehow flew past all of us waiting below at the monkey bars with outstretched gloves.

Even though I practiced all summer catching fly balls and I day-dreamed about it a lot, I never did get one of Mr. Kirk's towering shots in the web of my glove. But, there was always next summer. No ...I was sure I would be home by then. It would be up to Rocco and the other kids to worry about it.

I also started third grade. My teacher was Mr. Garrett. Usually he was nice, but sometimes the kids would get him mad if they were fooling around or fighting. When Mr. Garrett yelled, everyone shut up. Third grade at Whitford Training Center seemed a lot like the last few weeks of June when I finished up second grade. I didn't feel like I was going to get any F's on my report card. I made friends with a kid named George. He was one of the kids Mr. Garrett yelled at sometimes. George wasn't mean, but he talked a lot.

The first time I noticed George was in the summer when Mr. Kirk hit one of his long home runs. George waved his hands frantically back and forth above his head and loudly called for the ball.

"I got it ... I got it," he yelled.

He shuffled his feet a little to the left and in to adjust to the ball that was nose-diving to the ground. The other kids moved away from him. That's because everyone else realized the ball was flying way over George's head and right over the monkey bars. A few kids laughed at George, and he said, "Shut up, you jerk! I almost had it."

"Yeh, real close. What are you blind?" a kid called back.

After that, I noticed George always called for the ball, but he usually wasn't close to it. I didn't really talk to him in the summer, but now we started to become friends. George hung around with a kid named Harold, who was a big kid and kind of quiet. He usually didn't bother anyone, but I saw Harold get mad once outside and he grabbed one of the other kids and threw him to the ground. The counselors broke it up right away, and Harold got in a lot of trouble. Some of the kids said they locked him in a room by himself.

* * * *

Picture of Jar of Baked Beans
Fall 1964
Whitford Training Center

Dear Troy,

When I saw this picture I knew you would like it because you like beans so much. Next time I play football against you I'm going to squash you. See you soon.

love

dad

* * * *

Dad was always joking with all of us. He knew I hated baked beans. I made sure I didn't have those on my plate at Whitford. There was no way I was going to eat baked bears. Dad would always tell us how good we did when we were playing any sport. But he would also say, "I bet you can't hit this pitch," or "I'm gonna tackle you." That just made me want to do all the better and show him. And when I did, it felt so good. And I could tell he was happy for me, too.

Even though we had switched seasons to football, the major league baseball season was still going on. The schedule was winding down and the Yankees were in a tight race with the White Sox and the Orioles to win the American League pennant.

* * * *

Picture of Fishing Boats
October 3, 1964
Whitford Training Center

Hi Troy,

Mickey Mantle hit another home yesterday. If the Yankees win today, they will be the champs. I hope they win, don't you? I had a nice time visiting with you last Sunday. I can't hardly wait to see you next week.

Love

Dad

* * * *

The Yankees beat the Indians and clinched first place to win by one game over the White Sox and two over the Orioles. Even though we lived closer to Boston than New York, Dad and I rooted for the Yankees. I liked Mickey Mantle the best. Dad said the Red Sox players were spoiled. They got paid a lot of money and didn't really care if they won or lost. Harmon Killebrew was the home run king with 49 for the year. I wondered if he could hit the ball farther than Mr. Kirk.

The Cardinals beat the Yankees in the seventh game of the World Series. But we didn't get to watch the games or listen to them on the radio. Dad would tell me things about the games and the Yankee players on Visiting Day. And sometimes I would hear the counselors talking about it.

Because Mom was mad at her, Grandma never came to visit me or sent me letters. I was hoping that my other grandmother, Dad's mother, Grammie, and my aunt and uncle, Gloria and Will, and all their kids would come on Visiting Day. I asked Mom and Dad if Gloria and Will could visit, but Will's car wasn't good so they couldn't make it.

Sometimes Grammie wrote me letters or sent me a card.

* * * *

October 11, 1964

Hi Troy;

Just got through talking to your Dad on the phone. He told me that he had been up to see you this afternoon and you were getting along O.K.

I would love to get up there, too, to see you but it is so far away. Did you know that I moved to Rosewood last July? My father and i are living together. He needed someone to take care of him and so I quit my job (because I didn't feel good at the time but am fine now) so—left my house in Lansbury, and came down here. Next week, I'll take a trip to see Gloria and all her kids, but will have to make it short as Pa will have to have his meals.

Are you going to school and what grade are you

153

in? Is it third? Hope you like your teacher. My sister's girl is teaching the second grade down here and while she talks to her children trying to teach them, they raise their hands and want to tell her jokes. She really has fun but tries very hard to keep them quiet so she can teach them.

Hope you don't try to tell jokes to your teacher during class but then I guess you're too smart for that.

Do you play football or baseball? I suppose you make time for that especially baseball because I remember when you used to play with your Daddy down in the Powell ball park.

Could you write to me Troy, just a few lines so I will know how you are doing? If you would like me to send you anything just write and let me know or you could tell Daddy or Mommy and they would tell me. Well Troy, I hope to see you one of these days just to see how big and strong you are getting.

Love from Grammie

* * * *

I didn't know it, but Mom had been calling and writing the Youth Development Council, politicians, Catholic organizations and different agencies to try to get me out of Whitford Training Center starting just about from the time I got there. She wasn't going to stand by and do nothing when Whitford Training Center didn't have regular psychiatrists meeting with me every week, like Dr. Drake and other doctors had done, trying to figure out my problems. Here she and Dad had given up custody of me so I could get better treatment, and she didn't think the people at Whitford Training Center were doing anything for me.

When Mom didn't get the answers she wanted, she moved on to someone else. She wrote to Senator Thurman Albertson, Cardinal Leo Grooms, and Congressman Gill Jarvis pleading with them to help her get me the treatment I needed. She went into great detail in her letters, giving them the whole history of my problems and what she had done to help solve them.

Here is the response Mom got back from Cardinal Grooms.

* * * *

November 14, 1964

Dear Mrs. Kane,

I thank you for your long letter. I read it and re-read it.

I would be happy to do anything I possibly could for you but I am helpless since the little boy is no longer under your custody and is placed in an institution. If you had come to me before he was placed in the Whitman Training Center, I might have been able to help.

My heart goes out to the boy. I have had many experiences with other lads similar to the experiences you have had with Troy. All I can do for you and Troy at the present time is pray for you. That I will readily do. The enclosed spiritual bouquet card witnesses to Masses to be offered for you both. Since more things are wrought by prayer than this world dreams of and since the *mass is the highest form of prayer, I am confident these mementos will be beneficial to you both.*

Begging God's choicest blessings upon you and yours and assuring you that I would be pleased to be of service to you if it was within my power to do so, I am

Your devoted friend,

Cardinal Leo Grooms

Archbishop

* * * *

Mom wrote a persuasive, lengthy letter of almost 3,000 words to Congressman Jarvis. She discussed my difficulties beginning at age four with depression, irritability, destructiveness and hallucinations, balanced with my high I.Q. in the 140s and my potential. She detailed her struggles and sacrifices to get me proper treatment, including bringing me to court as a stubborn child. She placed blame on the administrators at Whitford Training Center for their lack of insight into what I really needed for treatment and ended with an emotional plea.

* * * *

For this reason, I appeal to you to help in any way you can to get for my son inpatient intensive psychiatric therapy.

I appreciate your patience at my lengthy missive and am enclosing a picture for you of Troy, who, aside from which ever potential he eventually realizes, is now and for only too brief a time, a little boy with a past and a present of sadness that was never meant to be part of the enchantment of childhood.

Sincerely,

Brenda Kane

* * * *

As a now eight-year old boy who was trying to fit in with the other kids at Whitford Training Center, I didn't know anything about what was happening regarding keeping me in Whitford or sending me to some other place. All I knew was that the Board met at the end of the month. I thought the only thing that mattered was me being good and staying out of trouble. Based on that, I hoped the Board would put me on the list to go home soon.

On November 6, I met again with Dr. Gifford, the psychiatrist for Whitford. Mr. Cranwell had told Mom and Dad when they met him on the first Visiting Sunday that the psychiatrist evaluated each boy within the first month that they came to Whitford Training Center, and then again at some point before they left the institution. So being interviewed by Dr. Gifford again might have been something they planned to do anyway, but more likely it was because Mom was calling and writing other people who might have been getting in touch with Mr. Cranwell about me.

Dr. Gifford was nice. I could tell he wasn't going to yell at me. We talked about how things were going at Whitford, and, just like before, about all the things that had happened when I was home. He never asked me about when Mom used to tie me into bed and smother me, and I didn't tell him about it. I did tell him that I got punished.

Sometimes when Dr. Gifford asked me a question, I could feel my face turning red and I felt embarrassed. It didn't even make that much difference what he asked, but I felt awkward, like everyone was all of a sudden looking at me even though I was just with him. That happened in class, too, when I had to read out loud, or when Mr. Garrett asked me a question. I hated that feeling, but I couldn't stop it.

I didn't know it, but Dr. Gifford wrote a summary of the interview and how he thought I was doing. Here is the report he wrote that explains his thoughts in detail.

* * * *

Troy Kane-Psychiatric Interview 11/6/64

On this date I interviewed Troy again-six months having elapsed since his arrival at Whitford Training Center in May of this year.

He is a fine appearing solidly built young eight year old, with striking brown eyes, and a lurking smile which he is ready to display if his conversational partner initiates it. He was alert, well oriented, disarmingly candid about difficult items, and showed a well developed sense of humor (reactive, not so much in the sense of creating it). He did not initiate conversational items, but answered rather quietly, but consistently all items I presented to him. Often, his face would redden with a flush, along with his verbal response to my questions.

Correlated reports from the Superintendent, Mr. Cranwell, and the JTC, Mrs. Griffin, indicate that Troy has been a model boy at Whitford Training Center, showing little or none of the notorious behavior which he manifested at home–destructiveness, assaultiveness toward younger brother, disobedience–which led to his commitment to the Youth Development Council as a "stubborn child". In school, he is doing satisfactory work at his grade level, as we would hope with his superior I.Q.

With respect to the past record, it is impressive that a series of clinical studies, done in a series of Mason Heights's most distinguished child-caring and evaluating facilities–have, sooner or later, been interrupted–apparently when Troy's mother feared that not enough was being done, or that some other facility might be better for him. It appears to me that some of Mason Heights's best individuals and their clinical facilities (child guidance and child psychiatric hospitals) have not had a fair try in helping Troy. I stress this because of indications that Mrs. Kane is, at the present time, making efforts to have Troy transferred from Whitford Training Center because he is not receiving formal psychotherapy. What I consider more impressive is the fact that the famous Whitford "milieu" therapy has provided Troy with the first six month period of model behavior and school progress of his recent career. It would be unfair to Troy, in my opinion, to interrupt this program of proven helpfulness.

The interview material with Troy reveals little that is new, or not already reflected in his clinical record. Perhaps because he has been interviewed by so many clinicians, he expresses directly that his problem is "jealousy of my brothers, so I started to hurt them". He claims that, by now, his mother has convinced him that she really loves him just the same as all his siblings, but Troy tempers this by observing that he "likes his brothers right after he gets home, then (he) soon starts not liking them again". Apparently this conviction given him by mother is only skin deep.

What is striking about his conversation is the coolness and lack of appropriate affect or compunction about his destructive acts–directed against his mother, sister, and brothers; family dog and cat, and the shingles of the house. His technique is a combination of marking and/or poking with razor or ball point pen (as on the knees and legs of his mother and furniture coverings his mother is making); slow slashing with a razor–(this eluded me, for I was unable to learn from Troy how he managed to leave a razor autograph on his mother and sister without waking them).

I was impressed by Troy's straightforward comments about his angers toward his parents (for locking him in his room, so he wouldn't hurt his brothers, so he crawled out on the roof and tore off the shingles).

It would be to the entire family's benefit, if the parents could match his candor. Troy's record is too, too perfect–of children training themselves, etc. His development milestones are within normal limits, but the development record reads too smoothly–with the surprising misbehavior (directed towards Doug) as if it were a surprise to all. Only as the fuller story comes in much later does it begin to appear that mother was quite harsh on penalizing and punishing Troy for his bitter resentment of Doug–a standard human reaction of human children. This points the

spotlight to mother and her self-understanding; hopefully, she will seek clinical help for herself with
the same energy she seeks it for Troy-so she can better understand the impact of her unhappy childhood
and whatever relationship it may have in respect to
her intolerance for the expression of anger of children toward their parents (and toward interlopers in
general).

I recommend that Troy remain at Whitford Training
Center from the long range viewpoint. He could return
home when mother's tendency to lateral pass, and project, and displace is replaced by insight about herself.
Otherwise, a long series of residential placements is
anticipated. Crystal Home could be considered, but not
before a full clinical period at Whitford has been
completed. Let us not naively deceive ourselves in
overestimating the need for "psychotherapy" as if it
were the only measure that could help Troy to succeed.

I have read mother's saga about her life with Troy, and
I feel that the kindest act in his behalf she could
make at this time is to give qualified persons in
proven places (Whitford Training Center) the opportunity to provide Troy with the constancy and security
which has been absent for the past several years of
his life. As some clinician said, sometimes the kindest
deed by a parent is to let the child go (into temporary
care of qualified persons). In my opinion, mother Kane
would be more attending to her own anxieties than
to Troy's welfare if she were to continue her agita-
tion to have him removed from Whitford-which she did
without really inquiring into the qualities of the
Training Center and its program. But only on the ba-

sis of surface consideration, namely, that it didn't have a psychiatrist in daily attendance who would provide psychotherapy for Troy.

Let me restate once more: the clinicians, individual, private, and in the employ of the State-know that psychotherapy is but one specific therapy in our therapeutic armamentarium. It works best when the conflict to be dealt with is an intrapsychic one. Troy's is not primarily such a problem.

In my opinion he needs the more total experience of "corrective emotional experience" as it can be provided through milieu therapy, in a setting of constancy and predictability, and where there are strong adults to identify with. I believe that Whitford Training Center can supply these better for Troy-168 hours per week, than could psychotherapy one, two, or three hours per week at best.

This does not preclude reviewing Troy's situation during the months and years ahead. At this time, a major change in his present situation does not seem indicated, in my opinion.

Respectfully,

Marcus Gifford, M.D.
Psychiatric Consultant
Whitford Training Center

* * * *

It was getting close to Thanksgiving, and I knew I had to stay at Whitford at least until the Board met again at the end of the month.

I wouldn't be home and my family couldn't visit on Thanksgiving because that was on a Thursday, not Visiting Sunday. Mom always made a big turkey on Thanksgiving, and called him Tom the Turkey. She got up really early and put him in the oven. She made stuffing that was like potatoes, but had pieces of the turkey in it that made it taste really good. She put pickles and olives in fancy dishes. I liked the pickles a lot.

I felt sad as one holiday was already lost, and soon it would be Christmas. I wanted nothing more than to be home. I hoped I would be back in Belport for Christmas and we could go see the decorations and lights in Mason Heights again like we did last year when I was home.

I couldn't understand why I had to stay at Whitford Training Center when I did everything they asked me to do. In school, I wrote a letter saying how hard I was trying. I hoped with all my heart that the Board noticed and would be telling me to pack my blue suit case soon.

* * * *

Mom continued to make calls and write letters. In December, she finally was able to talk directly to the head of the Youth Development Council, Dr. Lucy Hurley, who was in charge of my care and treatment. Mom wanted her to transfer me to the Evans Development Center, where they had full-time psychiatrists on staff who could give me the psychotherapy she said I needed.

At the time, I didn't even know that my mother had talked to the head of the whole Youth Development Council. Mom's notes about this call said that Dr. Hurley felt I was doing well at Whitford Training Center and that I would not be sent to Evans Development Center as it would ruin my life. Mom wrote that Dr. Hurley said *Mom wouldn't be happy until I was in a mental institution, and maybe Mom was the one that belonged there*. Mom also wrote that Dr.

Hurley said that I was under her care now, and to stop writing letters to people about the care and treatment I should be getting. It was up to the Youth Development Council to take care of me, and that is what they were doing.

It was probably good that I didn't know this was going on, because I would have been afraid that Dr. Hurley would be so mad at Mom that I would never have gotten out of Whitford Training Center.

In January, the whole issue of me leaving Whitford Training Center to get psychotherapy came to a conclusion. Congressman Jarvis followed up on Mom's letter to him and wanted to find out about my situation. The Assistant Commissioner of Evans Development Center spoke with Dr. Gifford about my case, and they decided it made sense for me to stay at Whitford Training Center. They sent a letter to Congressman Jarvis explaining what they decided about my care. Congressman Jarvis forwarded the letter to Mom to let her know what they decided, which she already knew by this time.

Of course, Mom wasn't satisfied, but there wasn't anything she could do in the near future. With me doing well at Whitford Training Center and the State in charge of my care, I was not going to be transferred to a different institution.

11
Snow Sledding

Although sleds had been used for centuries as a way of transporting people and goods through ice and snow, the roots of sledding as a sport took hold in Davos, Switzerland in 1883. An Australian student named George Robertson outraced 19 others over the four kilometer course to win what is considered to be the first international sled race. The next year, a 3/4 of a mile sled track, called Cresta Run, was built in St. Moritz. The racers lay on their backs on their sleds in a style now called luge racing, and navigated the 10 turns.

In 1887, racers on the Cresta Run track began lying on their stomachs on their sleds. This style became known as Cresta racing in honor of the venue. In 1890, a scaled down, bare bones sled designed for riding on your stomach was developed. This approach became known as skeleton racing. About the same time, bobsledding, which featured larger sleds and multiple riders, was developed. Bobsledding got its name from riders shifting and bobbing their bodies to gain more speed. Eventually, luge, skeleton and bobsledding became Winter Olympic events.

In the United States in 1889, Samuel Leeds Allen patented a recreational sled called the Flexible Flyer that you could ride sitting up or lying on your stomach. Riders could push the horizontal piece of wood attached to the sled's blades to steer it to the right or left.

The Flexible Flyer did not sell well when it was first introduced, but later it was marketed through toy departments in stores and sales took off. For kids in the US, during the winter, there was nothing like racing down a hill packed with snow on a Flexible Flyer.

* * * *

The week leading up to Thanksgiving was cold and in the twenties, and like flour making its way through a sifter, fine flakes of snow sprinkled the grounds. However, it was too early for winter. The snow that landed on the pavement melted immediately. But the white dusting on the grassy hills stuck around for a few hours and got all of us excited. Kids who had been at Whitford Training Center during the previous winter talked about all the snow storms we got and the great sledding down the hills.

* * * *

November 17, 1964

Dear Mom;

How are you feeling today? Fine, I hope. Will you ask Aunt Gloria and Uncle Will if they can come up to see me the 29 of November? I think that it is going to snow before next visiting Sunday. I think I am going to this board meeting. Well I hope I do.

How are Robin, Brian, Doug and Dad? I had a good time Sunday. I am trying to be good so I can come Home before Christmas.

Your loving son,

Troy Kane

SNOW SLEDDING

* * * *

As December rolled in with more cold and more snow, I really hoped I would get a sled for Christmas. I still wanted to be home, and I wanted to use my sled with Robin and my brothers, but if I was stuck at Whitford Training Center, I hoped I would get my own sled to go down their big hills. I had heard that there were only a few sleds to use at Whitford, and that the big kids took them. There were also metal flying saucers that didn't go as fast and you couldn't steer. It would still be fun coasting, but having my own sled would be a lot better.

When I was home, I really looked forward to Christmas. Mom would put up the decorations, like the manger scene, the green plastic holly and the chains of colored paper rings glued together. In the weeks leading up to Christmas, each night, Mom lit a special candle and we would sing Christmas carols while she played the piano. And of course like most kids, I could hardly wait to open my presents to see what I got.

About the only dream you could have at Whitford was that you would go home soon. At least that was what I thought about. But some kids didn't even talk about going home, maybe because they were used to being away or maybe because their families didn't come to see them on Visiting Day.

The Board met and I wasn't on their list for kids getting out of Whitford and on their way home for Christmas. I couldn't understand why the Board didn't like me, but I was getting used to life at Whitford. I had some friends. I did my best to stay away from the tough kids that might beat me up. I was doing good in school, and we got to go out and play sports. I didn't cry at night anymore. I wanted to leave Whitford Training Center, but I had learned how to live there.

Dad sent me a post card telling me about the whale that washed up right on the sand at Belport Beach. He and Brian were on the Channel 3 News standing near it. Boy they were lucky! I wished I had been there, then I could have seen the whale and been on TV, too. I wished I could have been watching them on TV so I could have bragged to George, but we never watched the news and didn't get to watch TV that much.

* * * *

Picture of Cocker Spaniels
December 17, 1964
Whitford Training Center

Dear Troy,

Doesn't the dog on the left look like Cinnamon? It's freezing today—just 15 degrees—and I'm on my way to meet Dad in Elkon. We're going to do some Christmas shopping before I go to work. I love the beads you gave me and the card was so nice I have it hanging in the parlor. Now I have to rush so I won't miss the bus.

Lots of love

Mom

* * * *

My mind drifted to last year when I was home for Christmas. We were so excited; Brian and I woke up early. Brian checked to see if Robin was awake yet. She was. So Robin went downstairs to ask Mom and Dad if we could all go downstairs and open our presents under the Christmas tree in the parlor. Robin was the oldest and she could be trusted not to peek at all the presents, so she got to go downstairs to talk to Mom and Dad. She came back upstairs and said, "Mom and Dad say it is still too early to go downstairs. We have to be quiet. They'll tell us when we can come down."

How could they not want to see what Santa brought?

Brian asked, "How long do we have to wait?"

"They said not too long, maybe 15 minutes," answered Robin. She had to act more grown up, but she was just as anxious to go downstairs.

While we were waiting, I thought I heard Santa's reindeer walking on our roof. That meant Santa was at our house. I tried to be really still because I didn't want him to know we were awake. He might not have left us our presents if he thought we might sneak a peek of him. We all waited at the top of the stairs for what seemed like forever; then finally Mom and Dad were awake. They called us and we all ran down the stairs, excited to open our presents.

Christmas morning at Whitford Training Center began like any other day, with Mr. Sullivan waking us all up. My friend, George, didn't feel like moving and stayed in bed.

Whack! Whack!

"I said move," Mr. Sullivan said in a firm voice.

Whack!

"I'm sorry, Mr. Sullivan," uttered George.

When Mr. Sullivan started slapping, everyone moved extra fast. The rest of us were ready for inspection when George slipped into line, his tears still dropping to the floor like melting icicles from the gutter.

I don't think George and Rocco and some of the other kids had warm Christmas memories to shield them from holiday loneliness. They got a few small things from the training school, but their parents didn't come to see them or bring presents.

My family was right on time. Mom had wrapped a big present for me. She said it was from Santa, but I knew it was from Mom and

Dad, and it looked big enough to be the sled I asked for. I tore off the wrapping paper. It was a sled, a Flexible Flyer!

It was mostly shiny black, with light gray and white trim. The runners on the bottom were painted red. What a beauty!

Even though there wasn't enough snow outside to go sledding, I lay down on top of my new Flexible Flyer right on the floor, and twisted and turned the handles that steered it. I figured before one of the counselors came over and yelled at me, I better get off of it. But all I could think about the rest of the day was trying it out.

* * * *

Picture of Exotic Garden
January 1, 1965
Whitford Training Center

Dear Troy,

As I write this, it's almost midnite and then it will be New Years 1965. I hope 1965 will be a good year for you and all of us. I have 3 days off from work and I need it. Saturday when I'm off, I'm sending you a package. Hope you will like what I send. Thanks for the nice letters. I love your letters—

and love you

Mom

* * * *

When you are eight years old, you don't really think about New Years or what a whole year is going to be like. About all I was thinking about was my new sled, but we didn't have much luck with the weather. It was cold, but we didn't get a lot of snow.

170

SNOW SLEDDING

* * * *

Whitford Training Center

January 12, 1965

Dear Mom;

How are you feeling today? Fine, I hope. Thank you for the tonic, popcorn, peanuts and thank you for bringing up my Phantom ship. Boy, I'm glad that it snowed.

I hope that there is not too much snow when you come up visiting Sunday. We might be able to go sledding today. I hope so because I have not used my sled yet, but first we will have to pack it down with the flying saucers. How are Robin, Brian, Doug and Dad?

Last test I got Ninety five, I think I'm passing. I hope so. Write soon. Love to all.

Your loving son,

Troy Kane

* * * *

Mr. Kirk said we would be going out in the afternoon to sled. Everyone was excited. Mom had given me a warm winter coat for Christmas. It had a soft, red lining that was smooth to touch.

Mr. Kirk got out the sleds and flying saucers. There weren't enough for everyone to have their own, so most of the younger kids had to wait until they could get a turn. I proudly stood with my Flexible Flyer propped up in front of me, as we listened to all the rules about where we could sled and how everyone had to take turns. I didn't have to share my sled, but I told George he could try it after I went first.

As we started to go towards the hill, an older boy asked me if I wanted him to pull my sled over to the hill. He surprised me and I was a little afraid of him, so I said, "Okay."

He grabbed the rope from my hands and pulled the sled through the deep snow. Mr. Kirk told the kids with flying saucers to go first to pack down the snow. Then it was our turn. The big kid lay down on my sled on his stomach.

"Hop on," he said.

"Um ... okay," I said.

I was disappointed that I couldn't try my new sled by myself. I was barely able to jump on his back before he started sliding through the fluffy snow. We raced down the steepest part of the hill. I held on tight. As we hit the bottom of the sharp incline, the sled dug in and we pushed down hard on the runners. I was glad I was not on the bottom because I would have been squished. The sled leveled out and headed up a bump and we soared through the air. Again we hit hard on the ground and all our weight pushed hard on the sled. We bounced a few more times and then the ride flattened out. We coasted way past everyone else and finally came to a stop.

Wow! What a ride.

The big kid said, "That was great! Let's do it again."

He grabbed the rope and started pulling the sled up the hill. I hurried along so he wouldn't go without me. As we climbed back up the steep part of the hill, I saw George standing there patiently.

"That was great," George said.

I could tell George wanted to give it a try, and I wanted him to feel how fast my new sled went. This time I wanted George and me to fly down the hill.

"Can George try it this time?" I asked the big kid.

I hoped he wouldn't get mad at me, but it was my sled and I wasn't really friends with this kid anyway. It didn't matter; either the big kid didn't understand that I wanted to ride down the hill with George or he didn't care.

The big kid said to George, "Sure, hop on."

He lay down on the sled on his stomach again.

"Come on, hurry up," he barked.

I pushed George to get on and George pulled me onto the sled on top of him to form a triple decker of bodies. We rocketed down the steep incline, like bobsledders who decided to try a new technique. As the hill flattened, suddenly gravity kicked in. Our three bodies pushed down hard on the red runners and the welded bond on the right runner gave way.

Snap!

My head jutted forward and my mouth hit the back of George's head. He did the same thing to the big kid underneath him. The runner dug into the snow and pitched us off the sled. We hit the snow hard and tipped over on our backs.

We barely had time to pick ourselves up when we heard, "Look out!"

A flying saucer almost steamrolled us as it bounced and slid past us.

I tipped my Flexible Flyer back on its runners, grabbed the rope, and tugged it out of the line of fire.

"Wow, that was something. Let's do it again," the big kid said.

"It's broke," said George.

The right runner had snapped under our weight. My sled was wrecked.

I wanted that sled so much, and it was ruined the first day I used it. I didn't want to tell Mom and Dad because I thought they would be mad at me. Mom wrote me asking if I was using the sled. I didn't say anything about it in my return letter. On Visiting Day, I finally had to admit the sled was broken when Mom asked me if I liked it. Mom and Dad didn't yell or look disappointed in me, but I felt really bad about it.

* * * *

Mr. Smith was an older, black man who swept the hallway floor outside our rooms, and then washed and waxed it at night. Sometimes, he used a big buffing machine that spun around and around on the bottom. It looked almost like he was dancing on ice as the machine slid from side to side and he seemed to glide right along with it while holding on to the handle. It looked like they had been practicing together for years.

After Mr. Smith and the machine moved past my door, I opened it and waved to him.

He turned the machine off.

"Well, look who it is. How's my buddy doing today?" he asked.

Mr. Smith even had a rhythm to his conversations.

"Good, Mr. Smith," I said.

"This part of the floor near your door needs a little extra care. Would you like to help?" he asked.

"Sure!" I answered.

"Well, come on over here and you and Bessie can waltz a little," he said.

He held the handle with me to get it started. It precisely swayed back and forth like a metronome until Mr. Smith let go. The machine darted to the left. I put all my weight on my left foot and pulled the handle to the right as hard as I could. The machine stopped going left, and started to drift right. I shuffled my feet to the right and suddenly we were dancing to the right. It started to pick up momentum, and now I dug my foot in to the right and pulled the handle left to stop the machine from hitting the wall.

Mr. Smith reached over my head and put his hands over the outside edges of the handle. The machine started doing what I wanted it to do. It floated back and forth with ease. Eventually, Mr. Smith let go of the handle and the machine added a few more spins before coming to a halt. He looked closely at the part we had been buffing.

"Well, look at that! Have you ever seen a shinier floor?" he asked.

A smile swept across my face, forming a small triangle, as my happiness peaked through like the sun breaking through on a cloudy day.

"You really have a knack for this," he said as he and Bessie waltzed back and forth on their way to the end of the hallway.

12
Deltiology

Postcards have been around at least since the 1800s in one form or another in many countries around the world, giving people a quick way to send a message to someone else. Early postcards often did not have any pictures on them. In 1873, U.S. Post Master John Creswell put the one-penny postcard, appropriately named for the one penny stamp pre-printed on it, into circulation. The U.S. government declared that they were the only ones in this country who could print postcards. It wasn't until 1898, when the Private Mailing Card Act was instituted, that the U.S. government relinquished its postcard printing monopoly.

In these early versions of postcards, people were required to write the address of the recipient on the back, and their message on the front. In the early 1900s, the government authorized divided-back postcards, which allowed the message and the address to be written on the same side. This opened the door to more creative designs, many of which were imported from Europe. In 1908, despite a population in the United States of 88 million, the U.S. Post Office handled 678 million postcards, an average of almost eight per person. As technology improved and colorful pictures were added, collecting postcards became a popular hobby known as deltiology.

* * * *

We had a new kid named Michael in our class. He was kind of quiet like me. We started to hang around together when we went outside. Michael didn't seem to belong at Whitford Training Center either. He wasn't one of those tough kids. He seemed like someone that I would have met at Brantfield or Children's Center.

Michael didn't really like sports, and he didn't do very well when Mr. Kirk got him to play baseball or kickball. Sometimes I felt bad for him, especially when some of the other kids made fun of him.

Michael had this strange habit of licking the outside of his mouth with his tongue. He did it quickly, in a circular motion like the hands of a clock going all the way around from 12 to 12 in just a second or two. At first, I noticed how much he did it, but then I didn't think about it anymore. I guess Michael didn't either. It was automatic, like breathing to him. He did it so much though that the skin around his mouth was red and dry. It formed a reddish-brown ring around his lips.

"Hey, lick this," scoffed one of the older boys.

"Looks like ring around the toilet bowl to me," laughed another big kid.

Michael looked sad, but he didn't say anything back to them. He wasn't a fighter. I hoped he wasn't going to cry.

I figured Michael must have felt like me when my face got red. I hated that feeling. The worst part about feeling embarrassed or having a ring around your mouth was that everyone could see it. If no one else could see that you licked your lips or you were embarrassed or didn't like talking in class, it wouldn't have been as bad.

The more I worried about my face turning red, the more it happened, especially in school. If Mr. Garrett asked me to read, I could feel the red flowing across my face. I was embarrassed to be embarrassed. I figured my life would have been so different if I could have somehow hidden my lack of confidence, because nobody else would have known it.

On the first day of spring, we got a little snow that stuck to the grass, but they weren't going to let everyone go sledding. Sometimes it seemed like the counselors said no just to show everyone they were in charge or maybe they just wanted to be mean. It melted quickly anyway.

* * * *

Picture of Gilmington Town Hall
March 1965
Whitford Training Center

Dear Troy,

We park where the car in the picture is parked when we're on our way to see you and go in a drug store across from the park and get your cans of tonic. There is a church on the left of the picture that was built in the 1700's. We will look at it together someday when we are bringing you <u>home</u> from there. The day will come Troy. I love you very much.

Love,

Mom

* * * *

I read this postcard a bunch of times, daydreaming about how it would be to go home, hopping in the station wagon between Mom and Dad in the front seat, and driving out of Whitford Training Center for good. It sure felt real when I played it out in my mind like that, but nobody had said anything about me really going home.

* * * *

Picture of Pearmont Stadium
April 1, 1965
Whitford Training Center

Dear Troy,

I'm all thru for the night and I'm glad. Tomorrow it's supposed to <u>snow</u>. Today was April Fool's day and Brian gave Dad a chocolate candy that looked real, but was made of rubber. Have to hurry home now. See you soon.

Lots of love

Mom

* * * *

Mom didn't talk to me about it, but she had been trying to get me placed somewhere else for a long time. Mom got a call from Mrs. Griffin and Mr. Wade from Whitford Training Center. Nobody told me anything about this either, but they wanted to talk about me going home.

Mom didn't understand how they could suggest that I could live at home. I had only met with the psychiatrist twice in the whole time I was at Whitford. Mom and Dad had given up custody of me, but Whitford Training Center didn't give me the treatment she thought I would get. Maybe feeling like she held the winning hand in a high-stakes poker game, Mom said I could come home but only if they saw to it that I got the clinical care and counseling I needed.

Mrs. Griffin said that there wasn't any need for me to get counseling. Mom wrote in her notes that the argument spiraled out of control as Mrs. Griffin said that all I needed was love.

Regardless of the details, there was a standstill. Mom still wanted me to get the counseling she said I needed, and the people at Whitford Training Center thought I was fine. I was still blindly going through my day-to-day life at Whitford Training Center, and hoping that the Board would see that I was being good and would send me home. The disagreement meant that I wasn't going home yet.

* * * *

Picture of Lighthouse
April 13, 1965
Whitford Training Center

Dear Troy,

This should make 149! And tomorrow's 150! That is some collection. Loved being outdoors with you Sunday and can hardly wait til next visit.

Lots of love

Mom

* * * *

As the days started to get longer and spring began to show its face with warmer days and rain, my postcard collection continued to grow. I was now up to 150 and counting.

* * * *

April 15, 1965

Dear Troy,

Tomorrow is Good Friday, the day of our Lord's death on the Cross. There are two things I always

180

think of on Good Friday, <u>One</u>—how much God the Father asked of His Son, Jesus, His life! <u>Two</u>—how much Jesus, His Son gave.—His life and in giving His life He gave us our lives, so that we may also live after death. And this gift of life after death is for <u>everyone</u> who believes that Jesus was God's son and the King of Heaven. Even this thief who was being crucified beside our Lord shared in the wonderful gift—because he believed. "Remember me Lord, when you come to Your Kingdom", he said. And Jesus was comforted because the thief believed Jesus was both God and man and Jesus told him "This day you shall live with Me in Paradise." No matter what wrong the thief had done in his life, because he cared, was sorry, <u>believed</u>, he went to heaven with Jesus.

On Easter morning we celebrate because Jesus was seen alive after he had been buried, cured all. His loved ones knew then that He had kept his promise and tho' His death on the Cross was hard for them to see, the sorrow was over when they knew He lived after death. And God the Father gave the world something beautiful that Easter—a promise of hope—that after the terrible sadness of Good Friday came the happiness of Easter. After trouble and sorrow, comes comfort and joy. I believe this and hope you will too. I love you very much and wish you the happiness of Easter and God's love for you always.

You have my love always Troy,

Mom

* * * *

Picture of Hanville Academy
May 1, 1965
Whitford Training Center

Dear Troy,

This is not far from where you are. I'm through work now and I'm glad. It's been a busy week. When you come home I'll bring you in and show you the department I work in. There are a lot of new buildings going up by the hospital and one of them will be a new part of the hospital. Watch for a pkg. in the mail.

Lots and lots of love

Mom

* * * *

Slater County Medical Center was a big and busy place, known for its medical research and top doctors. Mom was interested in medicine and would sometimes watch the operations in the observation area. She bragged that Slater County was one of the best hospitals around. She enjoyed medicine and being part of something that was important.

Because I was away from home so much, I had not gone to parochial school, like Robin and Brian did when we lived in Powell. My parents switched all of us to public school after we moved to Belport. I also hadn't gone to Sunday school like Robin and Brian did. The people at Whitford Training Center did try to make sure we went to mass and they also said we would soon receive the sacrament of Confirmation.

Usually, kids didn't get confirmed until they were in junior high, and I was only eight years old and in third grade. But that is what they told us. To be confirmed, we had to pick an additional name. So I was going to be Troy Lee _____Kane. It was kind of fun getting a new name.

My friend Michael and I talked about the Confirmation. I liked his name and he liked my name. You had to talk to your parents before you could pick a name, but Mom and Dad agreed Michael was a good name. So that was going to be my confirmation name.

* * * *

Picture of Three Cats and Milk
May 13, 1965
Whitford Training Center

Dear Troy,

Isn't this card cute? The middle one is like Rascal used to be.

Today we got paint for the living room. Dad and I are going to paint it light blue. Thank you for the nice letters you send me. I look forward to them every week. I'll see you soon. I love you very much.

Mom

* * * *

We always had cats. I don't know if Dad liked them that much, but Mom sure did. If a strange cat was hanging around the street, Mom would feed it. Before long, we had another member of the family. Rascal was one of our cats. I am not sure how we got him, but he had a shiny coat of striped fur. So we named him Mittens. He was always getting into something, so before long we called him Rascal.

Although he would sometimes play hard to get, Rascal liked being the center of attention. He even sat in the box with the colored wooden blocks we used to build houses and bridges. Sometimes, Robin would tie a string to the block box and pull him around the living room. Rascal looked like a proud lion you would see on TV, perched on rocks overlooking a grassy green meadow, although in reality he was sitting on top of the uncomfortable wooden blocks of various shapes and sizes. Robin would top it off by carefully placing an eraser on the top of his head between his pointy ears. As Rascal was transported around the floor, Robin and Brian would sing, "Here comes King Rascal, here comes King Rascal."

I could hardly wait to see the living room all fixed up, painted in light blue. I could picture Mom's blue stained glass lamp on the end table and the pictures of the old sailing ships at sea hanging on the walls of our new living room.

* * * *

Happiness is a thing called—You! card
May 1965

Hi Troy!

How are you? I'm dying to have you home again. I can hardly wait for summer. Dad and Mom bought a new rug and couch. The rug came, but the couch won't come for a couple of weeks. They have been painting the parlor and sunroom. We'll have a lot of fun at the beach. It's only about a month 'til summer. I'm looking forward to seeing you next visiting day.

Love,

Robin

DELTIOLOGY

* * * *

Then, finally, I got word that I would be going home. It wasn't going to happen right away. I would finish the school year first. Not exactly as I had played it out in my mind, but at least I was going home. I just had more time to build it up.

Soon, I could sleep in my own bed and wear my own clothes. Soon, I could sit on the new couch. Soon, I could go up the street to the beach and swim. Soon.

* * * *

Picture of Battleship
May 30, 1965
Whitford Training Center

Dear Troy,

I think the happiest news I've heard in a long time was the results of the board meeting. It gives us an awful lot to look forward to doesn't it? I'm very happy, and proud of you. I know how hard you've tried. We have tried hard too. And now ahead of us lies a happy occasion—you coming home! Life won't be perfect at home—because we aren't and you aren't—and only God is (perfect). But with God to help us, and with us all together, home will start being home again. And I'm looking forward to it—for there is nothing that can come up that our love for each other can't help us to work out O.K.

Lots of love

Mom

* * * *

I don't know what other conversations there were between Mom and people at Whitford Training Center, or if Dad was involved at all. But somehow they came to an agreement. I was going home after the school year ended. When I was home, it always seemed like things just happened no matter how hard I tried. I just kept getting in trouble. But at Whitford, I was able to do things right. Things were different now and I was sure they would be better when I went home, too.

The days didn't move fast enough for me, but it was now June. Every day, I checked my mail. I usually got a postcard or letter, and still sometimes even a package with snacks from Mom. I kept counting my postcards. I wanted to get to 200, but I didn't want to wait at Whitford Training Center any longer than I had to. So it was okay if I went home before reaching my target.

* * * *

Picture of Metropolitan Ave.
June 14, 1965
Whitford Training Center

Dear Troy,

We came by here on our way to see your Confirmation. We had to leave the house at 7 AM and when we got to Hanville each person we asked where the church was sent us in a different direction. But we finally made it and saw you receive the sacrament, which meant a great deal to me. I was so very proud of you and so grateful we could be with you on such a wonderful day.

My love always, little soldier.

Mom

DELTIOLOGY

* * * *

For my Confirmation, I got to wear a nice suit. It felt good to be spruced up when we went into the church. We all got a little plastic statue of Jesus. I was happy that my family came to see me. I was now Troy Lee Michael Kane. I had already practiced writing my new initials, T-L-M-K. It felt kind of funny having an extra name, but I liked it. My friend, Michael, added Troy as his confirmation name.

With the weather a lot warmer and the days longer, we started playing baseball at night after dinner again. It felt good to hear Mr. Johnson singing Moon River again. Mr. Kirk had a big smile on his face when he came to bat for the first time of the year. All the kids that had been there the summer before, turned and sprinted to the monkey bars. The new kids didn't know why. Sure enough, Mr. Kirk hit the ball right over the monkey bars on his first time up. I ran in and the ball went right over my head. Nobody caught it, and Mr. Kirk trotted around the bases as we all scrambled to get the ball and throw it towards home plate.

* * * *

June 22, 1965

Dear Mom;

How are Robin, Brian and you feeling today? Fine, I hope. I will be going home very, very soon. By the time you get this letter it will probably be time for me to go home. I can't wait to go to the beach. I thought I would never get home.

How are Doug and Dad? Do you know why I am so happy? Please will you tell me when you are going to take me home? I would like to know. I counted my post cards and Sunday I had 182 of them. God keep you close to Him always. Write soon. Love to all. I love you.

Your loving son,

Troy Kane

P.S. I will be waiting for you to come and get me.

* * * *

The school year ended at Whitford Training Center. I had passed and would be going on to fourth grade in the Roosevelt School in September. Unlike when I finished first grade and was going to live at home again, there was no talk this time about a double promotion. But I had done a lot better at Whitford Training Center, and didn't have to worry about staying back.

I woke up early on the day I was going home. This time, I had lived away from home for about a year and half. I didn't need Mr. Sullivan's wake-up call. We went outside for a little while after breakfast. It was hard to believe that I wouldn't be there anymore.

Mr. Kirk told me my family had arrived to pick me up.

"Heh, keep swinging away at that ball. We might see you playing in the big leagues some day," he said. He shook my hand like I was a grown up. I grabbed my blue suitcase, which had my 186 postcards and letters in it. Then we went to Mr. Cranwell's office.

My family rushed over to me and hugged me. Mr. Cranwell wished me good luck and said he didn't expect me to ever come back. We walked out the door and into Dad's station wagon. Dad drove slowly down the tree-lined winding driveway, past the tall cement pillars and onto Route 57. I was part of the family again.

On the way home, Mom wanted to stop at Slater County Medical Center so her friend, Vicki, could meet me. Vicki and Mom had become good friends. Mom had told Vicki all about me, and

Vicki would switch days with Mom sometimes to make sure she didn't miss Visiting Sundays.

We all went in to meet Vicki. Mom was glad that her boss, Mr. Wilton, wasn't there because he wouldn't have liked us all there when there was work to be done. Mom introduced Dad to Vicki.

"Now I know why Brenda makes such a fuss about you," Vicki said.

Then Mom introduced me to Vicki.

"Well, look at you. I knew right away you were Troy. And look at those rosy cheeks. Aren't you the handsome one," she said.

She was pretty like Mom had said and funny, telling us a few stories about her boyfriend, Little Eddie. Then we headed home. Two weeks short of my ninth birthday, I had spent 1/3 of my childhood in psychiatric wards, a mental institution, a juvenile detention center and a training school for juvenile delinquents. I was hoping I was home for good.

13
Dog Days of Summer

Although a cobbler by profession, John Augustus, born in 1785, had an interest in the legal system, and felt that petty thefts and public alcoholics were handled too harshly by the courts. More importantly, he felt that many of these people could overcome their problems if given a chance and guidance. One day while observing court proceedings in Boston as he often did, Augustus felt the destitute man before the judge, charged with public drinking, showed promise of reform. So he convinced the judge to let him take responsibility for the man and paid the man's bail out of his own pocket. Augustus helped the man overcome his alcoholism and got the man a job. When they returned weeks later to report to the court, the judge was so impressed he released the man.

With his ability to select people that he could help make positive change, Augustus had an exceptional success rate. The court allowed him to intervene on behalf of more and more people. In time, community leaders and organizations helped finance the bail for which Augustus was obligated to pay, because he was having such a positive influence on the community.

Augustus had a special place in his heart for children, and initially helped two girls and a boy, who had been caught stealing. The judge required Augustus to report each month on how the children were doing. If the children showed positive behavior for months, in what is now known as probation, the children would be free. Augustus took on more children from as young as seven to 16 years of age as a standard practice.

Before Augustus died in 1859, he had helped about 2,000 people in this manner, with only four forfeiting bail. In 1878, Boston passed a law, assigning a permanent probation officer to its court. This practice eventually was adopted across the country.

* * * *

"I think he's here," said Mom.

I peeked out the sun room window onto our street, and saw a man with a big sedan pull up close to the curb. He jumped out of the car, folder in hand, took a puff of his cigar and strode towards our house.

He was quickly up the front steps as Mom opened the door to greet him.

"Mrs. Kane?" he asked.

"Yes. Please call me Brenda and come on in," Mom said.

"Hi, I'm Mitch Landry from the Youth Development Council. Feel free to call me Mitch. I'm Troy's Educational Counselor," said Mr. Landry.

Dad stood behind Mom on the step leading into the living room. Dad smiled and Mr. Landry quickly reached out and firmly shook Dad's hand.

"Hi," said Mr. Landry.

"Hi. I'm Russ," said Dad.

"Well, this must be the good athlete I've been hearing about," Mr. Landry said as he turned towards me.

He reached out his hand and, like an experienced wrestler, locked up my hand with his. I wasn't used to shaking an adult's hand, but fortunately he smiled and released me. The smell from his cigar was strong, and the white smoke formed a puffy cloud that squiggled towards the beamed ceiling.

191

"Oh ... Let me put this out. Bad habit," he apologized. "Athletes don't smoke cigars, do they, Russ?"

"Um ... no," Dad quickly agreed.

"Let me get you an ash tray," said Mom.

She went to the kitchen and came back with an ash tray. Neither Mom nor Dad smoked. Mr. Landry smudged out the cigar, and rested it on the edge of the ash tray.

"As Troy's educational counselor, I will be keeping an eye on how Troy is doing. I will come by each week and talk to you and Troy. And I may take Troy out for a ride or something to get him out of the house and get to know him better. Maybe we can go to a ball game some time. How's that sound, Troy?" he asked, turning to me with a wide grin.

"Ah ... good," I said, but at the same time thinking I wasn't sure that I wanted to go somewhere with this man I didn't know.

"I think everything is going to go just fine, but if there are any problems, I want to know about them. I am here to help Troy, and you," he said.

"I have read Troy's history, so I know what the problems were in the past, and also how well he did at Whitford Training Center," he said and smiled at me. "The most important thing is Troy being part of the family again, and getting back to school."

Mr. Landry stayed for a while longer, and did most of the talking. I recalled some of the older kids at Whitford talking about their probation officers. That's what Mr. Landry was. He was my probation officer. I knew if I didn't do what Mr. Landry said, he would put me back in Whitford Training Center or maybe somewhere worse. I think Mom and Dad were a little worried about Mr. Landry, too. Even though he smiled and laughed when talking, Mr. Landry seemed like their boss, too.

"Well, I have a few more people to see. Don't forget about that ball game we're going to," he said to me and winked.

He shook our hands again, and then grabbed his folder and cigar and was out the door.

Even though I was home now, I got a few postcards that were reminders of life at Whitford Training Center.

* * * *

Picture of Old Dunes Beach
July 7, 1965

Dear Troy,

How is it at home? Did you get the letter I sent you last weekend? How is your family? Tell them I said hi. Well, I will write soon.

Your friend,

George

* * * *

Picture of Pink Flamingos
August 6, 1965

Dear Troy,

I'm finally back home after traveling some 5,689 miles. I toured the South and places of interest. My main interests were the Civil War Battlefield areas in Antietam in Maryland and Pennsylvania. I even collected some Civil War bullets. Plus much reading material to go along with that I have already collected.

Sincerely,

Mr. R. S. Kirk

* * * *

I wasn't entirely used to being back at home. At supper, sometimes I forgot and raised my hand to ask if I could have more milk or more food. Mom kept reminding me I didn't have to do that at home.

I kept to myself a lot, but one day we played school. Robin was the teacher, and she started to ask us to spell words. I felt so good when she asked me how to spell a word and I got it right. Things were going along well until Robin asked me how to spell the word, *ceiling*.

I wasn't sure, but I thought I spelled it right.

In a nice way, Robin pointed out my mistake and wrote it on the small blackboard to show all of us how to spell it. She wasn't mean or anything, but I felt really dumb. Now Robin and my brothers knew I wasn't that smart. Even though Robin tried to reassure me, I didn't want to play school anymore.

There were a lot of kids on our street to hang around with, but I didn't want to play with them. I didn't like trying to make new friends.

I either stayed in the house or played in our yard. Even when Brian or Doug tried to include me with their friends, I didn't want them to. They were their friends, not mine. And I was afraid that the kids in the neighborhood would find out why I had been away from home for so long. What if one of the kids asked me about it? What would I say?

I also knew that Pete Holcomb lived in Belport. He had gotten out of Whitford Training Center before I did. What if I saw him at the beach? What if I was with other kids and Pete Holcomb started talking to me about being at Whitford Training Center? What if he got caught stealing a car or something, and it came out that he and I had both been at Whitford and were juvenile delinquents?

About a week after we met Mr. Landry, he came back to see me. He wanted to talk to Mom and Dad first, so I had to go outside and play. Then he came out and asked me if I wanted to go get an ice cream. So we went for a ride in his fancy car. He drove a lot faster than Dad did, and it was fun sitting in the front seat and feeling the wind blowing in my face. He asked me how I was doing, and I said everything was good. I didn't want him to think anything was wrong. When he said that Mom and Dad were happy to have me home and there weren't any problems, I was relieved.

When we got to the ice cream place, he asked me what kind I wanted.

"Coffee," I said.

"Coffee ice cream?" he asked.

"Ya ... ah please," I stammered.

"I never heard of a kid having coffee ice cream," he quipped.

I told him that Mom had had coffee ice cream when she was pregnant with me. Mom said that I must have started liking it when I was just a baby.

"So Troy, what do you want to be when you grow up?" he asked.

I perked up and said, "I want to be a baseball player."

"I heard you were a good athlete," he said. "I wouldn't be surprised."

On the drive back home, Mr. Landry was puffing on his cigar and holding up both ends of the conversation. I was beginning to like him.

* * * *

Dad worked nights at the donut shop. Sometimes during the week, he brought home donuts, muffins and coffee rolls that were a day old. On the weekend, he often came through the door with two boxes of freshly-baked goods and two newspapers tucked under his arm. He had the opposite schedule from everyone else in

195

the house. He was the only baker at the donut shop and worked six nights a week to make all the donuts and pastries.

Before going to bed in the morning, he sat at the kitchen table and ate his breakfast. When he was hungry, he could quickly wash down a few donuts or four pieces of toast with jelly with a cup of instant coffee as he read the sports pages.

"Yankees lost to the Twins last night," said Dad.

"What was the score?" I asked.

"Six to five, Twins," he said.

Then he hesitated like there was more to come, as he deciphered the sports page and relayed the information, which used its own Morse code, in sudden bursts and pauses.

"The Yankees scored a run in the top of the ninth to go up 5 to 4.... With two outs in the bottom of the ninth, ... Killebrew hit a two-run homer to win it. Wow!" said Dad.

"Did Mantle get any hits?" I asked.

Dad checked the box score and said, "Ya. 2 for 4 with a walk, but he's not having a good season."

"The Yankees don't seem to have it this year. The Twins look tough. They have Killebrew and Oliva, and their pitching looks better.... Heh, here is the other sports page if you want to read about it," he said as he handed me the Mason Heights Gazette sports page and moved on to reading the Tribune.

Like other mornings, every now and then, Dad would pop his head up and tell me about something that happened in one of the games. Other times, I would tell him about a story I read. But a lot times, we just sat there quietly, sharing our love of baseball.

* * * *

The next time Mr. Landry came to our house, he asked, "Troy, have you ever been to Fenway Park to see a ball game?"

"No," I said.

"Well, how would like to go next week? The Red Sox are playing the Twins," he said.

A half smile broke across my face, almost like I was trying to hide how happy I really was. Did he mean I was going to see a real major league game at Fenway Park in Boston?

"Really? Ya ... ah ... sure," I stammered.

"You know, I think the Twins are in first, and they have Killebrew. He's a monster," Mr. Landry added.

"I know," I blurted out. "Last year he almost hit 50 home runs!"

"Well, I'll let your parents know when it is and what time I'll get you, but they already said it would be fine for you to go," he said.

I couldn't stop thinking about going to the game and what it would be like to be a professional baseball player. I had this piece of foam rubber that I used to hit with a wiffle ball bat in the back yard, playing out my own major league games by myself.

"Now batting for the Minnesota Twins, Harmon Killebrew—Killebrew," I said in my echoing, announcer voice.

I took my stance in the batter's box and tapped the bat on the makeshift home plate I had drawn in the dirt. I took a few half practice swings, trying to mimic Killebrew's powerful batting stroke. Then I tossed the foam rubber up in the air and took a big cut at it.

Smack!

"There's a long drive to left field! It's deep ... it's gone. Home run, Killebrew! And the Twins take an early lead," announced.

Somehow, the games always seemed to come down to the last inning and last out, with one of my heroes determining who won or lost the game with a single swing of my bat. I lost myself in the moment, hoping to get the key hit that won the game.

Now, I couldn't wait to go to my first real major league game. Each morning, I read the box scores of the Yankees, Red Sox and Twins' games.

"Dad, do you think I'll get Killebrew's autograph?" I asked.

"Well, maybe. It is hard to get autographs, but you might get lucky," Dad said, not wanting to disappoint me.

On the morning of the game, I shared my breakfast and the sports pages with Dad. Later, Mr. Landry picked me up for the long drive to Boston.

"There it is," said Mr. Landry as we approached Fenway Park, with its distinctive green walls and massive light towers rising in the distance.

We were early for the game. Mr. Landry handed our tickets to the man at the turnstile and then bought a program. We walked under the stadium and up the stairs to the opening in the stands that revealed Fenway Park. Everything seemed so big and perfect. The infield and outfield grass was plush and green. The dirt-lined home plate area, pitchers' mound and base paths looked like they had been painted on a canvas. The stands were sprinkled with fans, hoping to see batting practice and maybe get a souvenir ball before the game started. The left field wall stood high, with a net stretched across the back to catch any home runs hit there.

"Let's go down here," said Mr. Landry, snapping me out of my dazed state.

"Oh ... sure," I muttered.

We were on the first base side of the stands, near the beginning of right field. I followed Mr. Landry as he walked towards a group of people. Suddenly, I realized these weren't just fans, but there were major league ballplayers there, too.

"How you fellas doing?" Mr. Landry asked, making his way right up towards the front.

He shook hands with one of the players. Did he know him?

"Troy, say hello to Mr. Bill Monbouquette. He is one of the few players to ever throw a no-hitter," said Mr. Landry.

My heart was pounding. My face brightened and I struggled to say "hi".

"What's your name, son?" he asked.

"It is ... um ... Troy," I finally managed.

He took the program and signed his autograph.

"Thanks," I said, dumbfounded.

* * * *

Bill Monbouquette was born in Medford, less than 10 miles outside of Boston. In 1958, he fulfilled a boyhood dream of pitching in a major league baseball game for his hometown team, the Boston Red Sox. A gritty player with an average fastball, Monbo, as he was called by teammates, used his curveball, precise control and fierce competitiveness to eventually become the team's best starting pitcher in the early 1960s. A four-time all star and a 20-game winner in 1962, Monbo became best known for the no hitter he hurled against Early Wynn and the White Sox at Comiskey Park in Chicago on August 1, 1962.

The affable Monbouquette needed just one more out to reach a milestone that has happened less than 300 times in more than 11 million games in a sport dating back to 1875. There were two outs, and future Hall of Fame shortstop Luis Aparicio was the last obstacle. With two strikes on him, Aparicio tried to hold back his swing on a close pitch. It looked like his bat came across the plate and it was strike three. Umpire Bill McKinley didn't see it that way and ruled it wasn't a strike, bringing the count to one ball and two strikes. An irate Red Sox fan in the stands yelled that they shot the wrong McKinley, mockingly referring to the assassination of President McKinley. Monbo had to step off the mound as he tried to hold back his laughter. Then he put his game face back on, stepped back onto the rubber and struck out Aparicio on the next pitch to complete his no hitter.

When he was with the Red Sox, Monbouquette would round up some of his teammates and go to the Dana Farber Cancer Institute and try to cheer up the kids battling cancer. He said it made him feel grateful for his own healthy children and put the up and down nature of professional baseball in perspective. Later in life, Monbo would return to Dana Farber, but this time as a patient, where they were successful in getting his leukemia to go into remission.

* * * *

Mr. Landry puffed on his cigar and we headed to the concession stand. Mom and Dad had given me money, but Mr. Landry paid for my hot dog and Coke. He also bought me a small, souvenir wooden bat with the words, *Boston Red Sox* stamped on it. It was small, but to me it was the real thing.

In the game, Carl Yastrzemski hit a double, triple and home run for the Red Sox. The sudden explosion of cheers from the crowd made me want all the more to someday walk out onto this field and play in the big leagues. With the game was tied 3 to 3 after five innings, Harmon Killebrew led off the sixth. He had already knocked in a run with a single in the first. Killebrew launched a towering home run into the net in left field to put the Twins ahead. The fans weren't happy, but I was thrilled. One of my heroes had just done what he had done so many times in my backyard, hit a home run to put his team ahead.

The next day, I was out in my back yard, using my souvenir Red Sox bat to hit the foam rubber ball and imagining that Killebrew, Yastrzemski and my other heroes were hitting clutch home runs.

Perhaps as a sign of problems to come, in early August things started to turn for the worse for the first-place Twins. At breakfast, Dad told me that Killebrew had dislocated his elbow and would be out of action.

About the same time, our older dog, Cinnamon, a golden brown cocker spaniel, got sick and died.

Mom asked me a lot of questions about me poisoning Cinnamon, just like when she said that I had poisoned Uncle Sal's dog when we lived in Powell. I didn't poison either dog, but I felt really bad about Cinnamon dying and somehow guilty.

I had been home about two months. My roller coaster life was plunging downward again. I figured it wouldn't be long before I was shipped off to another institution.

* * * *

On Saturday mornings, sometimes Mom would try to catch up on cleaning the house, which could get pretty messy with four kids in the family and her working full time at Slater County. The clothes were piled half way up the curving cellar stairs, waiting to be washed, sorted, folded and put back into circulation. I learned not to put my clothes down the basement to be washed unless they were really dirty, because it was like a large sinkhole that gobbled up my socks, underwear, pants and polo shirts. My clothes disappeared down there and I might not see them again for months, if at all. I usually wore the same pants to school every day.

If Mom was in a good mood on Saturday mornings, she would play her records and do some cleaning. She liked Patsy Cline a lot, especially her big hit, Crazy. Mom would sing along as Patsy Cline pulled us in with her emotional country twang. I sang along quietly to myself.

We all had chores to do, like cleaning our rooms, or sweeping the parlor or kitchen floors, or doing the dishes. We didn't do much dusting, as we had bigger cleaning challenges. During the middle of this, sometimes Mom would sing or maybe do a funny dance with a broom. She joked that our neighbors across the street could see her carrying on her histrionics. She might even shuffle along towards the sun room window like Charlie Chaplin, with her feet turned out sideways, and tip her make-believe felt derby to them and take a bow.

When Mom wasn't as happy, the house got messier and everyone had to be careful. Sometimes, Mom would spank us with the
metal shovel if she got mad. Unlike a hand with flesh and bones,
the shovel had no give and each strike inflicted intense pain.

Mom talked to Mr. Landry about me going to a psychiatrist. So
as the warm days of summer spent swimming at the beach turned
to the cool days of September and October, colored leaves and going to school, there was suddenly talk of me visiting the Haston
Mental Health Center. I had heard similar things before I went to
Children's Center in Mason Heights and the mental hospital in
Brantfield and the court in Scottboro where Mom and Dad turned
me over to the State. This time I wasn't going to have to stay there
overnight, at least not in the beginning, but the plan was for me to
see a psychiatrist for therapy.

It turned out that before I could go to the Haston Mental Health
Center and receive therapy, I had to have a brain wave test. No big
deal; I had a bunch of these over the years. Mom brought me to
Slater County Medical Center, where she worked, for my EEG. At
the follow-up appointment, we met with a pediatric neurologist,
Dr. Goff, to look at the results of my EEG.

Mom told her about my long history, starting when I was two
and held my breath until I turned blue. Mom said that sometimes
my body would twitch on one side and she wasn't sure if I was
conscious or not. She told Dr. Goff that my siblings had seen me
have a seizure and said that a neighbor had witnessed it once, too,
although she and Dad had never seen me have a seizure. This testi-
mony had become part of the history that Mom recited each time
we saw a new doctor, even if it wasn't true. She also recounted a
time when I seemed to lose consciousness and my head fell into my
hot chocolate, burning my face. I didn't say anything, but that was
something new she added and had never happened. She ended
with concerns about my continued destructiveness at home and

how she was worried when she left the house, because she didn't know what I would do to my brothers.

Dr. Goff told us that my EEG was slightly abnormal. It could mean that I might be more likely to have seizures or act out, but not necessarily. She said she would try putting me on medication as a precaution, and considered it to be a trial period, but the main thing was making me part of the family again.

So that night, I started a routine that lasted until I went away to college. I took two pills, 200 milligrams of Dilantin, before I went to bed.

I didn't feel any different after I took my pills. I was still the same me. But things changed .... a lot. That is a *drastic* understatement! It was as if all the things that I was accused of doing, all the time in hospitals and institutions where I wondered if I could ever come home and be part of the family again, had vanished. A magic wand had transformed my world. Mom said how things had changed since I started taking my medicine. In Mom's eyes, the eyes that really mattered, I was cured, as long as I continued to take my medicine.

When I woke up each morning, I didn't have to explain to Mom what I had done while everyone else was sleeping. I stopped getting in trouble. At first, it was such a relief. But how could I be sure it would stay that way? After all, each time I came home from whatever place I had gone to, problems surfaced again fairly quickly.

So even though Mom said things were better, I couldn't be sure. After all, I hadn't done anything differently to change things. They just got better. So I was expecting my life to just change back to the problems again. Maybe it would happen tomorrow or maybe the next day, but I figured everything would go back to the way it had been sooner or later.

In the following months, the improvement continued. I even got to play Little League baseball for the first time.

Mr. Landry kept coming by the house for his visits, and would often come to my games, and he noted the positive changes in his status report that he shared with Dr. Goff: "Subject's overall adjustment and behavior pattern has continued to improve. During the past eight months we have encountered very serious difficulties on the one hand; however, Troy seems to have developed the necessary threshold in order to help himself adjust to the stress situations in the home."

* * * *

Everyone was happier. Dr. Goff had figured it out. She gave me medicine that somehow must have changed me, and changed life for me and my family.

At the same time, I resented hearing Mom say that the medicine had cured me. There were all those things in the past she said I had done. I didn't believe they were true. And as I got older, I knew that Mom made up some of the stuff she said. Like she would add some details to the story or tell it differently when we went to see a different doctor, and usually ended it by crying. I knew she lied, and now she was so happy I was better.

But it was more than just that I was better; it was like Mom was the one who suffered and persevered, and made it happen. She had been continually frustrated in her quest to get me the right treatment, to make me better. She had brought me to Children's Center a bunch of times for emergencies when she said things were out of control. She argued with the doctors and administrators from Brantfield Mental Health Institute. They weren't doing the right things to make me better. Then Mom and Dad agreed to bring me in front of the juvenile court system as a stubborn child, and agreed to give the State custody of me. She said this was all done in the hopes of getting me the treatment I needed. And when it didn't work out, Mom didn't stop. She wrote to politicians and

Cardinal Grooms, she called institutions and brought me to see a series of doctors.

Now that journey was finally over. Mom said she felt sorry for all that I had gone through and that no child should have to go through so much. And she would do some things differently if she had it to do over, but it was worth everything we had gone through because I was better.

Although I was happy that I could live at home and get back to a regular life, I wasn't sure what had really happened over the last five years.

The whole thing about only having problems at home still didn't make sense. If there was something wrong with me and I did these horrible things when I was home, then I should have done the same bad things when I was away. If I was mentally ill and hallucinating at home, then I should have still been mentally ill and hallucinating when I went away. If I had seizures when I was home, then I should have had seizures when I was away. How could I turn it on and turn it off? How come I didn't have any problems when was away from home, even though I wasn't taking any medication? And then the whole thing about me doing things in the middle of night when I was locked in my bedroom and tied into bed was impossible.

Although I had been the disturbed kid who had been institutionalized in a mental hospital and juvenile detention centers, and I wasn't sure of all the details of my strange childhood, I didn't think the pills had any effect on me. And as I settled into this new, more normal life, I started to believe there had never been anything wrong with me.

14
Resiliency

In 2009 in the United States, there were three million reports of child abuse, involving approximately six million kids. That works out to be an average of one report of child abuse being made every 10 seconds. Sadly, it is estimated that more than five kids die each day from abuse. And of course, there are many cases of child abuse that go unnoticed and unreported, due to the victim's shame, guilt and fear and the abuser's intimidation and guile.

The tragedy of child abuse is not only the horrible experiences to the victims of the abuse itself, which can come in many forms, such as emotional, physical, sexual and neglect. It is also the long-term impact it has on the victims as they try to overcome these difficulties and attain a somewhat normal life. Unfortunately, statistics show that abused children often struggle and lead difficult lives. Abused and neglected children are 11 times more likely to get arrested as juveniles for criminal activity, and to struggle with delinquency, teen pregnancy, poor academic performance, drug use and mental health issues. And it is estimated that approximately one-third of the victims continue the cycle of abuse with their own children.

Despite these odds, some kids are able to rebound from these awful experiences and get their lives on track. Their resiliency depends on a lot of factors, including personal characteristics of the victim, such as self-esteem, confidence, intelligence, optimism, humor and independence. Other factors include influence from role models and mentors, the quality of their school systems, who their peers are and finding ways to focus their energies in a posi- tive direction. Even for the kids who are fortunate to find a way to turn their personal hell into something more positive, the course of their lives has changed forever.

* * * *

Despite the mental torture I endured of lying in bed with my hands and feet tied waiting for Mom to come into the bedroom and possibly smother me, or being forced to swallow a heaping spoon- ful of black pepper, or the bruises I got from my mother hitting me, I can't say that I ever thought of myself as being an abused child. Regardless, I learned not to stay in the past or dwell on what I couldn't control. I accepted the bad and the disheartening, not because I was noble or courageous, but because I had no choice. I just learned to look ahead and expect things would get better. I remained generally upbeat and hopeful, while at the same time pensive and cautious.

It was a September morning in 1966, and nature was trying to decide if it was summer or fall. As we made our way up the street towards the ocean wall with our shiny new shoes and pressed out- fits, speckles of the glistening sun had been carefully placed on the bluish-green water canvas. Robin was off to her first year of high school, Brian was beginning junior high and Mom was going to walk Doug and me to the Roosevelt School. We had first day jitters, but we were excited about the start of the school year.

Like Canada geese flapping and trying to get into their V forma- tion, our strides had slightly different lengths and our line was not quite straight, but we marched together. I made sure to step on the circular, metal water and manhole covers spread along our path. I considered the small ones good for a single, the cement driveway cornerstones weren't metal so they were only good for a walk, but the big manhole covers were home runs as part of the mental base-ball game I brought with me whenever I walked or ran anywhere. I tried to space my steps so I wouldn't have to break stride. Doug was doing it, too, and careful not to step on the lines that formed the sidewalk blocks we followed up our street, and then along Atlantic Boulevard towards the school. As we stretched out our new shoes with each stride, there was dog mess scattered all along the way on the sidewalk, left over from owners taking their dogs for early-morning strolls.

"Watch out," Mom said as we made our way through the dungy minefield.

"Be careful," she said.

"Don't step there."

Looking down at the shiny new penny I had centered in the small, leather opening on the top of my new, brown loafers, I was careful to avoid the dog mess. Our walk became sort of a game, as we hopped along and altered our strides to keep our shoes pristine.

"Be careful where you step, little boys," Mom said in a sing-song voice.

It wasn't long before Mom composed an impromptu song on our journey, and began to sing it.

Be careful where you step, little boys,
Be careful where you step, little boys,
Cause the dogs did their duty,
And they sure did some beauties,
So be careful where you step, little boys.

We all laughed as we made our way to school. Mom repeated it again and we all started to sing along and laugh.

After about a year of taking my medicine and not getting in any trouble, I started to believe that maybe I was home to stay. It wasn't a feeling that came to me suddenly one day; it was gradual. It crept into my thoughts and then I got used to being home and became comfortable with the idea.

Mom didn't usually scold or punish me, certainly not like she did with Brian. And really, she seldom had reason to as I was careful not to get in trouble because I didn't want to have to go away again. It was like she and I had declared a truce without ever discussing it. However, although our family of six lived in a small house, I managed to keep my distance from her, at least emotionally. I didn't consciously plan out this strategy, but that's how it ended up.

In spite of the unofficial detente, sometimes Mom's emotions and mine collided. Like gushing water freed from a dam, my pent-up resentment flowed freely and powerfully when it started to go down that path. Briefly, the hurt inside me escaped, the emotion palpable. I remember one time in particular, although I am not sure exactly what caused it. I got in trouble for something and Mom scolded me. I was fuming mad at her. In my mind, it didn't matter if I deserved it or not.

Who was she to tell me I had done something wrong? She had done a lot worse to me and never said she was sorry. Those horrible things had become our secret, although we never agreed that it should be kept quiet. We just never talked about what really happened, and no one else knew anything about it. She apologized for other parts of my childhood, saying how sorry she was that I had to live away from home, but always noted she had tried as hard as she could to get me the right treatment. And then she would end it all by crying, every time. I really hated it when she did that. I was the one that had to live away from home; I also had endured mental and physical torture at her hands, but it always turned into me having to make her feel better.

"It's okay, Mom. Don't cry," I always said.

But after she reprimanded me this time, it struck a nerve. I didn't talk back to Mom; I found a better way to get back at her. I ignored her. I acted like she wasn't there at all. I didn't say anything to her. It was a little awkward at first, but I didn't care. I was determined not to give in and act nice to her, even if she decided to be nice to me. I hadn't really thought it through, but it was working perfectly. She couldn't punish me, because I wasn't really doing anything wrong, and it let me silently lash out at her.

So that is how it started. After an hour or two, I stopped sulking, but I didn't say anything to Mom or even look at her, because I didn't want to make eye contact. I was still mad, and I was starting to enjoy what I was doing. I was happy when I made it through the rest of the night without talking to her. I took my two pills and went to bed.

The next morning began just as the previous night ended. I didn't talk to Mom or even look at her. I went about everything else the same as I normally did. I talked to Dad, and Robin and Brian and Doug like nothing happened or was going on. This contrast made my strategy all the more effective. She was the only one not in my world. As the day continued, I knew it was getting to her, and it felt good to have power over Mom for once. By late afternoon, Mom must have talked to Dad about what I was doing, or maybe Dad just noticed and decided it should stop. I'm not sure what made him step in, but Dad pulled me aside and talked to me about how I was treating my mother. He said that it wasn't fair to hold a grudge, and I was hurting Mom's feelings. He asked me to stop my silent treatment and start talking to her again.

Dad didn't yell at me or punish me. I knew I had to do what Dad had asked me to do, but still he was nice about it. I also realized my silent treatment couldn't go on forever, but it was a watershed moment for me. Although it was just for a few hours, I had been the one in control.

I didn't have to live in daily fear of being sent away. Chestnut

Ave. was now my permanent home. I was shy, lacked confidence and did not know how to make friends. However, I was getting a second chance at childhood. For Robin, who had been thrust into the role of pseudo mother and housekeeper and was now 15 years old, there was no bringing back her childhood. The same thing could be said for Brian, now a teenager with a somewhat tarnished outlook on family life. For Doug, the memories of threats of violence and long rides on Visiting Sundays to see his older brother in one institution or another, faded in time and were replaced with a mostly happy childhood. Years later as adults, Doug would tell funny stories about a childhood that reflected a very different attitude and experiences from Robin, Brian and me.

* * * *

One day, I was deep into one of my pretend Red Sox games in my backyard. I hit the foam rubber ball over the bushes for a game-winning home run. As I jogged around the bases, engulfed in my mind's happy ending, I heard people out in front of the Petersen house, diagonally across the street from ours. When the Petersens moved out, I went through the neat old stuff they put out on the sidewalk to be carted away. I found some post cards from the early 1900s, revealing that in their younger days, the Petersens had travelled all around the US, vacationed in Bermuda and even went to Paris. The US post cards had penny stamps on them. It had cost two cents to show their family and friends a picture of Paris and share what they were seeing and doing there.

Now it was time for another family to settle in and begin their story on Chestnut Ave. I curiously looked on from the backyard, tucked behind the corner of our house. I saw the parents and a few older girls. There was also a boy who looked like he was about my age. As they carried things into their new home, I sneaked through our front door without them seeing me.

"There are some people moving into Petersen's old house," I announced.

Later in the day, the new boy saw me in my driveway and came over to say hi. For some reason, I refused tell him my name or say anything to him. Eventually, he gave up and went back into his house.

It took a few days, but I finally relented and told the boy who I was and my age. It wasn't long before we were pitching the foam rubber ball to each other or playing catch.

Dave became my first close friend outside of an institution. As time went on, we started playing all kinds of sports together on our street with the neighborhood kids. Both of us could run faster and throw a football or a baseball better than the other kids. As much as we were friends, I wanted to do better than Dave whenever we played anything. I wanted to run faster or strike him out when we played wiffle ball or beat him in football. I don't know if everyone else kept track of how many times they won or lost, but I always did. I hated to lose.

But it wasn't just about trying to win. As time went on, I felt different when I was outside running around and playing any sport; my anxieties and inhibitions temporarily disappeared. I was a different person. As my confidence grew, I began to organize a lot of the games, knocking on kids' doors, gathering them up and helping to pick the teams.

* * * *

In the late 1960s, a can't miss hockey player named Bobby Orr caught the imagination of practically every kid in the northeast. He was just 18 when he joined the Bruins, but he quickly showed why the team had signed him as a 14-year old. Orr played defense and instead of just being content to stop the other team from scoring, he was the team's best offensive threat as well. He led the league in scoring twice while playing defense, which forever changed the way people thought about and played that position. And for people who had never shown any interest in hockey, like my mother and father and me, it all changed with Orr.

And while he was the NHL's most dynamic star on the ice, he was shy off of it. He avoided interviews with the press, and seemed uncomfortable talking about himself. And when he scored, he shared a brief recognition of the goal with his teammates and then unassumingly skated back to his position to begin playing again, as if he was uncomfortable about being as good as he was.

Although I still loved baseball, I now dreamed about being the next Bobby Orr. He was everything I wanted to be as a hockey player and I could relate to his quiet, unassuming nature. On Saturday mornings, Mom would wake me up at 5 a.m. I would walk to a neighbor's house in the cold and the dark, half suited up in my hockey gear to catch a ride to a youth hockey practice taking place two towns away since Belport didn't have its own ice rink. I wasn't old enough or good enough to skate with the kids on the big rink, so I practiced on the smaller crowded rink in the back of the building. It didn't matter. I was playing hockey.

The town also flooded the tennis courts at the high school during the winter months to give kids a chance to skate. We would play pick-up games, using our sneakers as temporary goals, or I would practice stickhandling with the puck through the sea of moving kids or shoot pucks at the chain-link fence, pretending I was playing in the Boston Garden with Orr and the Bruins. I went there after school and all day on weekends. At night, Mr. Lang would come to scrape the ice and then spray a light coating of water over the top of the ice. As the water sprayed everywhere through the big hose and gusty winds, he didn't seem to notice his icicle eyebrows or soaking hands and feet. Mr. Lang didn't get paid to do this. He just did it to give us a fresh, glistening surface for the next day's games.

He knew all the regular's names of the kids that skated at the tennis courts and tried to make us all feel like rising superstars. He borrowed from one of the big names in the NHL at the time, Frank Maholovich, known as the Big M.

"Heh, there's the Big K," he'd say as he saw me skate by. "You're looking good. Keep skating. Skate, skate, skate!"

In the eighth grade, I went out for the junior high hockey team. I decided to try out as a defenseman since I could skate backwards, and probably, okay definitely, because I wanted to be like Bobby Orr of the Bruins. I made the team, but didn't get into game action very often. It wasn't much different in ninth grade either, as I worked hard at my skating drills in practice, but mostly watched the other kids on the team play in the games. Sure, I wanted to get in the games, but it didn't dampen my love of hockey.

Eventually, I switched to playing forward, which was a better match for my skills. I worked my way up through the Belport Youth Hockey league, and then was invited to play with the Belport traveling team with the best players in our town that played other cities. After nervously waiting in front of my house for a ride to my first game with the travel team, a big car pulled up. I flung my equipment in the trunk and got in the back seat.

"Heh, here's the Big K," said Mr. Lang.

I smiled and settled in. In the coming months, I established myself as a solid player on the team. I knew I could play with these kids.

* * * *

Christmas was a big deal in our house. Mom set up the nativity scene, complete with the puffy white cotton serving as a 6" by 8" blanket of snow nestled in the manger. Mom strewed the plastic holly around the handrail and balusters on the stairs. The skinny pine tree, with more of its tiny needles jumping to the floor as each day passed, was covered with shiny plastic ornaments and the annual school holiday projects each of us had crafted, from faded construction paper, dried gobs of glue and shiny sprinkled specks. The tinsel, which held the warm colors from the strings of lights, was wrapped around the branches to keep the cats from chewing it. The white plastic star, outlined in red, sat atop the sapling and brought character to our tree.

Mom covered the kitchen table with flour, used her rolling pin to flatten the cookie dough, and out jumped Santa and reindeer cookies from the metal molds into the oven. The assembly line continued as Robin painted on Santa's suit and Rudolph's nose and lay them down to dry. My brothers and I did our part by washing down any overdone cookies or broken appendages with tall glasses of cold milk. The smell of the batches of Mom's tasty Christmas cookies made it tough not to reach in and take a few extras when the cooks weren't looking.

Each night, Mom played Christmas carols on the piano in the chilly sun room, as we made our way through all the selections. Dad was trying to get some sleep before he went off to the donut shop, but usually the rest of us were involved. We sang O Come All Ye Faithful, Mom's favorite, in English and Latin. The funniest part was when we sang O Holy Night and the lyrics called out, "Fall on Your Knees". I tried hard not to let Mom know I was laughing when Brian or Doug dropped to their knees when we sang that part.

Before Mom would begin a new song, she would point out whose favorite it was. Mine was Silent Night. I had even learned the first two verses at school in French. After we finished all the songs or Mom got exasperated at the fooling around, one of us got to blow out the Christmas candle. Similar to the fresh new ice surface freezing on the tennis court, the melted pools of wax from the night's activity formed a pristine seal until Mom lit the candle the next night to start the festivities all over again.

Of course, we kids were more interested in getting presents than worrying about the warmth of our holiday traditions. Although my parents didn't have a lot of extra money, Mom made sure each of us had a few special presents waiting for us under the tree from Santa.

But as Christmas morning shifted away from the excitement of opening our presents, I felt a sadness drift in like a dense fog coming in off the ocean. It wasn't that I didn't get good presents or that anything had gone wrong. And maybe that was it. Everything was good, but at the same time I couldn't hold back the memories of the deep sadness and pain I felt from all the years when Christmas had not really been Christmas for me.

* * * *

The high school was just a short walk from my house. At first, it was a scary place, as I was starting all over again as part of the youngest class in the school. The juniors and seniors were bigger and seemed a lot older than the lowly sophomores were. My strategy was to be quiet and try not to be noticed.

It wasn't just that I was low on the totem pole in school. I still wasn't entirely comfortable with my past and myself. After all, I had had all kinds of issues to deal with since I was younger. I had lived in a mental institution. My parents had given up custody of me. I had been sent away from home to live in a training school for juvenile delinquents. I had been tied into bed and smothered by my own mother. I still took medicine every night, linking my past with the present. Despite wanting to ignore all this, these were things I still thought about often and shaped who I was.

I lived in a dual world. One side was the quiet, but friendly kid that did well in school and loved to play sports. The other side was the reflective, introspective kid that still was dealing with a difficult childhood and a secret I was ashamed of and tenaciously guarded.

By this point, I thought that my past had been a mistake, but still the experiences I went through had dented my self-confidence. Consciously, I didn't think there had ever been anything wrong with me and I figured I was like all the other kids, but inwardly what I went through had changed how I looked at myself and acted.

By summer, there was a group of girls hanging around in our neighborhood and at the beach wall at the top of our street. I started to feel a little more confident, and began going out with a girl named Joan who was more outgoing and spontaneous than I was. Well, I guess that was to be expected, because I was so quiet, but I fed off her self-confidence and social nature. She met my parents and they really liked her. My mother was always complementing Joan on her cute outfits, and they would sometimes kiss and hug each other when Joan arrived or when we left to go somewhere.

I hadn't realized it before then, but suddenly it hit me. I didn't kiss my mother. I mean I *never* kissed my mother or hugged her. I wasn't intentionally trying to be mean to her, and I hadn't really noticed it before then, but I wasn't affectionate with her. And here was my girlfriend kissing my mother, and Mom smiling and taking it all in. If you were a casual bystander, you would have thought my girlfriend and my mother were family, and I was the outsider. It took me back to the whole crazy situation of when I was always in trouble and had to live in institutions and the horrible abuse I endured from my mother. In some ways, those memories were distant, but they obviously still shaped how I felt about my mother. I may have tried to act like nothing had happened and things were normal, but this realization dug up deep emotions I had tried to bury.

* * * *

At the start of my junior year, we had a new hockey coach, Coach Byers. The varsity team from the previous year had graduated a lot of talented players, who had made it to the coveted Metro Regional

Tournament as one of the best teams in the area. We were starting over with mostly new, younger players. I worked hard and did well in the tryouts, and made the team. Going into our first exhibition game, I was on the third line, which meant I would probably only get one or two shifts on the ice. We played Timberlake Academy, a powerhouse team, who dominated play. With just about two minutes left in the game, Coach Byers put the third line into the game for the first time.

I jumped over the boards like I was shot out of a cannon. I got the puck and blasted it into Timberlake Academy's end. I chased down the puck and hit their defenseman along the boards and got knocked down. I got back up and skated hard to catch up with the player I was covering. I skated as hard and fast as I could for those two minutes, bouncing off the opposition and instantly moving on to the next target like I was in the middle of a pinball game and I was the ball. I made such an impression on Coach that I went from barely playing on the third line to starting on the first line, where I remained for the rest of my high school days.

Going into my senior year, the town of Belport had built its own hockey rink. Unlike the previous year when we practiced at six in the morning in nearby Scottboro before school, now we would practice at three in the afternoon in our town in our brand new rink. It was fitting that the rink was dedicated to Mr. Lang, who had done so much for youth hockey in Belport, and had shown interest in me. Mr. Lang was the man who scraped the ice at the tennis court and sprayed a coating of water over it so the kids would have smooth ice each day. It was Mr. Lang who was the Big L of Belport Youth Hockey, and he wanted nothing in return, except for kids to skate, skate, skate and play the game the right way.

We had high hopes for the team, as most of the kids had played on our summer league team that dominated play against some of the teams we would play in the season. Coach Byers warned us about being overconfident, but some of our players began to tune out that message as he continued to remind us.

The first real game of the season was in Belport, and was the first home game we ever had. As I skated out onto the ice with my teammates to the roar of our crowd, Mom and Dad were standing near the entrance, waving with enthusiasm.

"H-e-h, Tr-oy," Mom called out.

We beat Orton Hill easily, 5-0. As smooth as the first game was, the second game was the opposite, as we lost decisively, 5 to 1. More significantly, our leading scorer from the year before and captain, Travis Mullen, suffered a serious injury, breaking h s collar- bone when he tried to overpower a defenseman along the boards. Coach talked to us again after the game about this defeat maybe bringing us back to earth, and he said in the press that he hoped we had learned a good lesson after our first loss. The teams in the conference were well-balanced. We had a good team, but we were one of five teams with legitimate hopes for winning the conference championship.

At the half-way mark in the season in late January, we were in second place, and anxiously awaiting our next game at home against first place Albertson. To avoid falling further behind them in the standings, we needed to knock them off. Albertson was by far the most explosive offensive team in the conference. Our team relied more on hustle, strong goaltending, and solid defense.

There was a deafening roar from our home crowd as the public address announcer introduced our team as we took the ice. But just 23 seconds into the game, Dotson, a tall center iceman from Albertson with a knack for scoring, put one past our goalie, Craig Conway.

Despite giving up the early goal, our line and the entire team controlled the play in the first period, outshooting Albertson 15 to 5. Their goalie somehow managed to keep us scoreless, although at one point we put six rapid-fire shots on him in just 15 seconds like a boxer does to an opponent that is dazed and leaning on the ropes.

As we came out of the locker room for the start of the second period, we were confident that we would put some shots past their goaltender. But when Albertson scored two more quick goals to put them up 3 to 0, things didn't look good. Before the end of the period, I stole the puck from their defenseman and fired a slap shot over their goaltender's right shoulder to put us on the scoreboard. After two periods, we were down 3-1.

The pattern for scoring goals in the first minute of the period continued in the final period, but this time it was our turn. The capacity crowd erupted with a loud ovation when I passed the puck to my linemate, Eddy Blanchard, and he blasted it past the goaltender at 15 seconds of the final frame to make it 3-2. Both goalies managed to keep the puck out of the net until with just over three minutes to play, talented sophomore Will Bartlett put the puck through the Albertson defenseman's legs and slipped the puck past their startled goalkeeper to pull us even at 3-3. The noise was deafening as our home crowd cheered wildly for our comeback, and hoped for more.

With a minute and a half to go in the contest, I passed the puck to Jim Roth and he shot the puck past their goaltender to put us ahead for the first time at 4-3. The noise was deafening. We held on to win, although I got hit in the face with a stick in the final minute of play, breaking my nose and requiring 25 stitches to close the gash over my eye.

After the game, Coach lauded my hard work and determination to the local sportswriter, saying I was the finest all-around hockey player he had ever coached.

Before the next game, I was able to buy a clear, Plexiglas shield, which covered my eyes and nose. It fogged up sometimes because of the cold air in the rink and my warm breath, but it gave me protection and allowed me to see everything on the ice.

Later in the season we played against another top team, Stover. Dad was the baker at a donut shop in Elkon and worked with one of the mothers of a top player for Stover. Although they were polite to each other, the rivalry was strong in the store, as the parents pulled for their sons. Stover had surprised us the first time we played them at their rink. With first place on the line, we were looking to avenge that loss.

With just two minutes to go in the first period, the woman's son from the donut shop scored to put Stover ahead 1-0. He scored again early in the second period to help his team build a 3-0 advantage, but we scored the next four goals with Blanchard and me getting one each and Bartlett adding two. After two periods, we were ahead 4-3. In the final period, I added another goal to boost our lead to two goals, but they countered with two quick goals to tie the game. Then with just 13 seconds left to play, the roof lifted off Lang Arena as Bartlett received a pass from Sloan, split the defense and faked the goalie out before sliding the puck past him.

As we came off the ice and made our way through the excited crowd to the locker room, I noticed Mr. Landry, my former probation officer who had been so helpful to me when I first got out of Whitford Training Center. I hadn't seen him in years. He was wearing a big smile like a proud father. We shook hands, his grip as strong as ever.

"Great game out there," he said.

We spoke for a few minutes, as players and fans shuffled past us. We only talked about the present, but I knew his influence had helped me get control of my life and a chance at opportunities like this.

To finish in first place, we needed to win our last game against Albertson, at their home rink. Both goaltenders were at the top of their games, making one save after another to keep the game scoreless. As the clock ticked off the final seconds in the second period, I swung around the net and tucked the puck past their goalie; however, the referee ruled that the buzzer sounded and time had run out just before the puck went in.

So after two periods, the game was still scoreless. The third period continued with the same furious pace. Then as the third period clock ticked down to the final minute, Albertson scored the winner and sent us plummeting to third place in the conference.

Even though the game had produced great theatre for fans of both teams, the outcome was really disappointing to us. We had come so close. The good news was that the season wasn't over. We had qualified for the Metro Regional Tournament. With so many good teams in the tournament, we would be considered an underdog in most matchups. One loss and we would be eliminated; however, we weren't done yet.

In the Mason Heights Sunday Gazette, sportswriter Jim Macie gave his assessment of the teams to watch. He predicted perennial power and Belfast conference co-champ, Camville, would easily defeat Belport and move on to the next round. Timberlake Academy was considered one of the favorites to win it all.

Coach cut out the Gazette article and circled the part about Belport losing in the first round, and blew it up into a five-foot poster. Before the game against Camville, Coach had our captain, Travis Mullen, who had healed from his broken collarbone, read how we were expected to lose. The team was pumped up as we took the ice in Hooper Lake, a town about 30 miles northwest of Belport, before an enthusiastic crowd of about 2,000.

The first period went as the experts predicted, with Camville controlling the play, but with one exception. They were not able to put any of their 13 shots past our goaltender, Conway. The score was tied 1 to 1 halfway through the final period, when Travis Mullen snapped a 10-foot wrist shot past the startled Camville goalie and we led again, 2-1. It was a wild finish, but when the buzzer sounded, we had prevailed. The write-up of the game in the Gazette the following day said it all, "For Belport, a hockey upset; for Gazette, a red-faced assist."

With the win, we advanced to the next round and were pitted against Casey, the Shoreline League champion and the team that Gazette sportswriter Macie had predicted would battle with Camville in the second round. Albertson, the team that beat us to win our conference, had also won their first game in the tournament and was matched up against Perryfield, the second place team in the Shoreline League. Albertson played their game just before us, and were thrashed, losing 11-1.

Now it was our turn to take the ice against Casey, the team that beat out Perryfield in their league. Casey had a high-scoring first line, so we knew we would have our hands full. Again, we relied on our goaltender, who kept us even at one goal apiece until late in the contest, although Perryfield outshot us.

In the final six minutes of the third period, we got three penalties. Despite the frenetic pressure in our end, Conway and the rest of our team managed to keep the puck out of our net. So at the end of three periods, the score was tied at one. There were no ties in the tournament. Someone had to win, so we were going to play overtime. First team to score would win.

In the first minute of overtime, Conway made a save and one of their forwards got a penalty for slashing our goaltender with his stick, which gave us the man advantage. We got the puck into their end and tried to gain control. It slid back to our defenseman, Carl Sloan, who fired a low slap shot towards the goal. I was positioned in line with the net and saw the puck heading toward their goal. I reached out with my stick and deflected the puck, changing its speed and direction. As the goalie moved his right leg to kick out the shot, the ricocheted puck instead went between his pads and across the red line into the goal. Our fans banged on the

Plexiglas and screamed and clapped loudly. I skated towards Sloan and jumped in the air, as he wrapped his arms around me in a bear hug. I soon found myself at the bottom of the pile of screaming, smiling teammates. My emotions were still racing, as we started to get ready to shake hands with the other team. We began to pick up our sticks and gloves, which were scattered all over the ice. It took a few minutes, but I found my helmet. My Plexiglas protective shield was barely attached, and was now on backwards.

Coach said he had a feeling we would win the game, and that it was his greatest thrill as a coach. Jim Macie of the Gazette jumped on the Belport bandwagon in his write-up of the game, pointing out our improbable run from a third-place team in a conference that was considered weak to knocking off two strong teams. He talked about our tight-knit team, our strong goaltending and our overtime win.

There was my picture in the two Mason Heights newspaper sports pages, the Gazette and the Tribune, celebrating the victory and my winning goal. These were the papers that reviewed the sports scene each day that Dad and I had routinely talked about since I was just a little kid. And now we were going to travel to play our next game at the Boston Garden, where the Bruins' Orr and Esposito played.

The tournament had started with 51 hopeful teams, some with much better chances than others, at least on paper. Somehow, small town Belport had managed to advance to the final eight teams. Everywhere I went, people were talking about the team and encouraging us. At school, all the hockey players were like celebrities.

We were slated to play against Timberlake Academy. It was an interesting twist of fate. Timberlake was the team who had easily beaten us in the opening exhibition game the year before when I was buried on the bench as a spare player until the very last shift of the game. I had improved a lot as a player in the last two years, and so had many of my teammates. We hoped for a different result.

When we came out onto the Boston Garden ice before the game, I glanced up at the crowd of nearly 11,000 people. Normally I could easily see my parents and other people I knew, but the individual faces were lost in the sea of screaming fans. It was thrilling. We set the tone in the opening minutes, hitting their players every chance we got. Conway continued his solid, and, at times, spectacular play in goal for us, ensuring that they would have to earn every score they got.

We held them to one goal in the first period, but the deficit had grown to 4-0 after two periods. We were disappointed, as we waited in the locker room for the third period to start. I didn't want this incredible ride to end. And we had our pride; nobody was going to beat us badly.

We didn't let down in the third period, and I blasted a long slapshot from the blue line that beat their goalie and pulled us closer at 4-1. Neither team scored again. We were out of the tournament. Timberlake Academy easily went on to win the championship, but we got some satisfaction that nobody played them tougher than we did.

While I was no Bobby Orr, I got to live the life of a high school athlete and enjoy some success. My hours of weightlifting, running and practicing had paid off, but more importantly, my love of sports had helped me channel my energies, gain self-confidence and build positive memories.

15
Questions, Answers and Hindsight

Munchausen's syndrome is a disorder where a person pretends to be ill when that person is in fact healthy, seemingly to get sympathy and attention. Along the same lines, Munchausen by Proxy (MBP) involves a caretaker, almost always the mother, deceiving medical staff into thinking that something is wrong with her child. The mother may cause physical ailments or build a case with the medical staff that her child is physically unhealthy or emotionally disturbed when that isn't true. There are often aspects to the case that do not add up and make solving the child's problem difficult, such as the dramatic difference in the child's condition in the hospital or facility versus at home.

MBP was first reported in the late 1970s by an Englishman, Dr. Roy Meadow, who described two cases in which the mothers had faked illnesses in their children. In one case, the mother had repeatedly altered and switched her child's blood samples, which made it appear that eight different antibiotic medicines had not worked to cure her child's illness.

With MBP, sometimes the mother may work in the health care field and have knowledge that she uses to make the deception more complex and difficult to detect. Often, the MBP mother exhibits an earnestness and active involvement in her child's care that may at first appear as the antithesis of someone who would create this false concern. And since it is the mother describing the problems of her young child, if anything, the medical community is not likely to suspect her of intentionally fabricating the illness. After all, why would a parent do that? The answer to that question is not entirely known, but it is believed to center on the mother's desire for attention and affection, drawing on the sympathy she gets from others who express their sorrow in her plight. It also seems to involve the motivation of deceiving people in authority who are considered experts.

A study by Sheridan in 2003 compiled information on 451 MBP cases, revealing the following statistics:

- Average age of the diagnosed child was four years old, with 75% under six years of age
- For cases that resulted in death, the cause was most often apnea, a common result of smothering
- Reported fake illnesses included feeding and eating disorders (24.6%), seizures (17.5%) and asthma, allergies and fever (each about 9%)

The end result is that MBP may be the most lethal form of child abuse, with an estimated 10% of the children dying. Of the children that survive, they are left with physical and emotional scars. Some victims later fall into the pattern of deception themselves, craving attention at any cost and faking their own illnesses. An aspect of the situation, which can make it difficult for the victims to truly understand what occurred, is that some of them may be ignorant of, or at the very least, confused about their mother's deception. Since these children are usually young, they may not know, or be able to comprehend, that their illnesses were fabricated by their own mother.

* * * *

At the time of this writing, I am an adult in my fifties, which means that not only is my childhood decades behind me, but also that I have had time to come to terms with what happened and build my life. Although I have chronicled my unusual childhood, I realize there is still much left that is untold. Equipped with perspective and hindsight, I want to fill in some of these gaps.

* * * *

Why did your mother do what she did to you? Why did she pick you out of your siblings?

I believe my mother suffered from Munchausen by Proxy (MBP), a mental illness that played out in unusual ways. I was a young and innocent victim, although I don't think my mother targeted me because she disliked me or because of anything I specifically did. My mother played the doctors, family and friends for sympathy, yet at the same time, seemingly took pleasure in fooling them. I don't know if the manipulations were conscious decisions, or if she was also deluding herself about my supposed illnesses. I tend to think it was a combination of the two. Whatever the machinations were, she was quite convincing. And since she came across as a very concerned mother, in tune with my supposed difficulties, the natural thing to do was to rely on what she said. Not only were many of the doctors and psychiatrists fooled, but I was to some degree as well.

And truth be told, my sister and older brother were not entirely spared punishment from my mother's volatile nature during this time. However, my best guess of why I was singled out as being ill is that I was also the right age at that time, young and vulnerable. When she started taking me to doctors to solve my supposed strange behavior and seizure disorder, my guess is that she liked the attention and it made her feel important, but I can't totally explain why she acted as she did.

* * * *

Why did your mother stop what she was doing to you?

My mother finally stopped targeting me when I was about nine or 10 years old. I am not positive why. In reading over her letters and post cards from when I was away at Whitford Training Center, I think she really did want to have a normal, happy family life. Without acknowledging her part in what was going on, she certainly said that was what she wanted. There were also several things working against her keeping this pretense of my mental and physical illnesses going. Since I was older, I was physically bigger and more aware of my surroundings. She would not have been able to tie me into bed or hold me down like she had in the past. I had demonstrated for several years that none of her claims of my bizarre and destructive behavior happened when I was away from home. A growing number of administrators and others at institutions I lived at did not think there was anything wrong with me.

I suspect that my probation officer being involved in our lives was also a strong deterrent. He was not someone to be taken lightly. He was persistent and would have been in the middle of everything if things continued to be out of control at home. I am sure he would have asked me directly what was going on and, by that point in time, I probably would have confided in him. Also, Robin and Brian were older and may have raised the issue with my father and others.

Possibly, outside of these external factors, my mother's motivation or thinking may have also changed. I really don't know. One thing I am sure of is that when my medicine supposedly cured me, the ploy of my supposed mental illness and potential seizure activity ended. My mother clung to her version of my difficult childhood, but she never again presented me as ill to doctors.

* * * *

How did you figure out what had happened?

I didn't quite have it all mapped out when I was going through it, but over time I came to realize that much of what my mother said about things I had done and my illnesses had to be wrong. When I went away from home to the mental institution and juvenile detention center and was out of her control, I didn't have the seizures she said I had; I wasn't violent; I never got in any trouble. What she said I did all the time at home did not happen when I away. *Ever.* When doctors and administrators didn't believe her, she tried to move me to other doctors and institutions to begin all over.

When I started taking my two pills each night before going to bed, I was just hoping that I would be able to stay at home. I separated my mother's smothering me and abuse from figuring out why I had to live away from home. The physical and mental torture experiences were deeply ingrained in my memory and made me anxious just thinking about them. They were real and palpable. However, coming to understand my mother's murky role in my supposed illnesses and the need to live away from home defied a normal mother-child bond of love and trust, and took me much longer to decipher.

Knowing that some things were not right was still very different from believing my mother was not telling the truth and responsible for what happened to me. However, I am introspective by nature, and went over things in my mind quite a bit. I recognized some of the stories my mother told the doctors were outright lies and other things she said just didn't match up with what I experienced. She had a way of making things sound dramatic and could be quite persuasive. In my heart I knew she was wrong, but initially I didn't consider that she made things up. I just thought she didn't have it right. At the same time, I wanted to bury my past instead of constantly reliving it in my mind and having to hide it from the other kids.

However, every day of my life going forward has been influenced to some extent by what I went through. So over the years, I thought about it and realized how far-fetched some of her claims had been. How could I have untied myself and unlocked the bedroom door and then sliced my sister's and mother's legs with a razor blade without them even waking up? How could I have climbed out the bedroom window and onto the roof in the dark and ripped up shingles? How could I have gone down the basement, grabbed a hammer and hit my brother in the head with it while he slept? And if I did do this, why wasn't he injured? How could I have done these things and then slid the deadbolt lock on the outside of the door from inside the room and tied myself back into bed? But most importantly, how could I have done these things and not realized I was doing *any of them*?

The further I got away from my childhood, the more I distanced myself in my mind from those painful memories. When I had to fill out a form when I went to the doctor's office, I would not check off that I had a history of epilepsy. I don't believe it is true. I didn't know all the details about what had happened when I was younger, but I knew my mother had been somehow responsible. I became increasingly skeptical of her.

After I was married, my wife and my sister on separate occasions told me about Munchausen by Proxy, which I had never heard of until then. My wife had seen a TV documentary on it, where a mother had been making her child sick and intentionally tricking the doctors who were trying to figure out the child's mysterious illness. My sister, a psychologist, suggested I read a book about Munchausen by Proxy by Dr. Marc Feldman called <u>Patient or Pretender: Inside the Strange World of Factitious Disorders</u> that chronicled this illness. The connection between Munchausen by Proxy and my past quickly became obvious. There was a name for what my mother had done to me. Although I had known that my mother was responsible for much of my bizarre childhood and could be quite manipulative, I had never realized she *intentionally* lied and the extent of her deceptions.

When I decided to write this book, I reviewed some of the documents from the medical staff who were involved in my treatment when I was a child, my mother's personal notes and my letters and post cards from my childhood that I had saved. It was clear to me how calculated my mother's actions had been. It wasn't just a big misunderstanding or a mistake; I was the victim of an unusual, bizarre deception that seemingly had no boundaries.

* * * *

Did you ever confront your mother about her role in your childhood?

One of the ways I adapted to the trauma I experienced as a child was to repress the emotional impact on me. So although my mother had physically and mentally abused me, I kept this inside me. And while I also held her responsible for me having to be incarcerated, I didn't lash out at her. It was just my personal belief. As an adult, when the whole picture of what happened became more clear, I was angry but still not sure if I wanted to confront her.

Sure I was upset, but I didn't want to give her the opportunity to lie some more and turn the whole thing into a big emotional meltdown about all she had done to get me help. I believed it would divide our extended family, as my younger brother and his wife and kids did not have any idea of what my mother had done and would have had to choose who to believe and what to do with this alarming revelation. The other factor was that maybe I repress a lot emotionally or maybe it is just the way I am, but I am not a confrontational person. What possible good could come out of me getting into a big argument with my mother at this point in my life?

When I decided to write this book and share my experiences with others, I felt it was necessary for me to discuss with her what I believed had happened, and tell her about my book. By that point, my mother was older and had been diagnosed with Alzheimer's disease. I told her that I didn't believe there had ever been anything wrong with me and talked about the horrible experiences of her smothering me. In general, she redirected the conversation and did not take responsibility for her actions. I wasn't combative and I wasn't looking for any particular reaction from her so I tried to end the conversation.

At that point, she became remorseful for my difficult childhood and her being so punitive. She did not really acknowledge fabricating my illnesses and I don't know that she could recall our conversation afterwards. If we had had this talk years earlier, I am sure she would have been furious. Either way, I don't know that discussing the past with her earlier would have been any more productive.

* * * *

The book focuses on what your mother did. What role did your father play in what happened?

This is perhaps the biggest mystery to me and a source of personal sadness. My father is no longer alive and we never talked much about my childhood problems, and certainly never his feelings about it or his role in getting me treatment. He wasn't the type to talk about things like that and I never directly asked him.

With our mutual love of sports, I always shared a bond with my father. As a child, I idolized him. When I became an adult and thought more about his part in my childhood, I have to admit I was disappointed.

When I was a kid, my father always treated me well and my mother did not hurt me when he was around. I don't know what conversations my parents had about my mother's insistence about my illnesses and need for treatment, but my father at the very least always took us to see the doctors and went along with bringing me to court as a stubborn child and giving up custody of me to the State.

If he questioned what my mother said about me, sadly, he did not assert himself, and seemingly went along with her. My father was not expressive and outwardly emotional like my mother. I suspect he did have some doubts about her claims, but did not follow through on inconsistencies about her claims that he must have noticed when he was around. Although my father did not lie about me to the doctors, he deferred to my mother. He took the easier path of going along with what my mother said.

Despite his acquiescence, I still like to think of the happy times with my father teaching me to play baseball, telling me jokes and sharing the sports pages with me at breakfast.

* * * *

You kept your mother's abuse of you a secret. Why didn't you tell someone?

It is a strange dynamic when you are a young child and your mother is punishing you excessively, and then goes beyond that. I am not sure why I complied with her. I guess part of it was because I was a young kid and she was my mother. But I didn't assess the pros and cons of telling someone what she was doing.

I certainly was afraid of my mother and I knew what happened when she got angry. I'm not sure I consciously thought about it, but if I did, I would have had to weigh heavily what would have happened when she found out what I had said. I just accepted her punishing me as part of my life. Of course I didn't like it, but I didn't think there was an alternative. In hindsight, it seems like it was an obvious thing to at least tell my father or the doctors. Maybe they could have done something. I am not saying it was a good decision, but I know I am not alone in accepting my fate in an abusive relationship.

* * * *

After being released from Whitford Training Center just before turning nine, you returned home, where you lived with your family until you went away to college. How did you reconcile those early years, maintain a relationship with your mother and achieve some sense of normalcy?

I certainly did not have any master plan in the beginning. I was hoping to get through the day without being hurt and hoping to stay at home. I wanted to be part of my family. It took some time to come to fruition and for me to believe it was permanent, but it did happen.

In retrospect, I tried to please others and be liked and fit in. I focused on the present. Maybe that was how my mind protected me from the past. And I don't want to make it sound like it was a calculated approach. It just happened.

I didn't think about my relationship with my mother, but it seemed normal to me. I loved my mother. She didn't hit me or harm me anymore, and I think she tried hard to care for me and love me. While it felt good to be loved by my mother, it also made me feel uncomfortable. I had resentment and anger built up inside me, although I didn't realize it, that drove me to keep my distance emotionally from her. I didn't want to be in a vulnerable position with her ever again. But not showing emotion towards my mother was not a conscious choice or a way to punish her. It was my natural reaction to her and my intuitive way of protecting myself from more pain.

As I strived for a normal life, I developed my sense of who I was and would become. Pragmatic, positive, easy to get along with, yet with an underneath layer that was introspective, thinking a lot about the people in my life and my level of comfort. I seldom reacted spontaneously, instead holding back and seemingly considering what I should do before I committed to anything. And as I detailed earlier in the book, sports was my outlet, my opportunity to expand my world, temporarily shed my inhibitions and have fun.

* * * *

This story focused on your childhood and adolescence. How has your life played out since then?

I am glad to say that I have been able to work through my childhood experiences and go on to live a fulfilling life. Like many kids with dreams of becoming a star athlete, I hoped I would be good enough to be a pro. After graduating from high school, there weren't any college coaches recruiting me to play hockey for their schools. So I went to a prep school, hoping to get another year of hockey experience and get noticed by a college coach. I made the hockey team, but did not come close to enjoying the success I had in high school. However, I worked hard on my academics and ended up being valedictorian of my class. I got accepted to an Ivy League school, a long way from first grade in a mental institution and second and third grade in a juvenile detention center.

My hope was to play varsity hockey in college, but I wasn't fast enough, skilled enough or big enough to beat out the other kids. I ended up playing four years of junior varsity hockey. Given how much sports meant to me, it was frustrating because I wanted to play varsity Division 1 hockey, but I still loved the game so I continued playing. Academically, I really struggled. I felt intimidated by kids who were outwardly much more confident than me and seemed smarter. In some instances, I didn't have the background to do the work, such as when I took Physics for Scientists and Engineers as a freshman. Big mistake. I never should have listened to my advisor on that one.

I didn't distinguish myself in the classroom, but I was able to graduate with a degree in Psychology. I worked briefly in the field after graduation, but didn't enjoy it and didn't feel like I was making much of an impact. While trying to decide what was next for me, I did some painting and construction work.

One of my jobs was putting in large replacement windows in an office building across the street from Children's Center in Mason Heights, where my journey to institutions as a child began. While coming in from the window ledge on the fourth floor back into the lab in a pediatrician's office, I accidentally stepped on the faucet in the sink and snapped it, sending water flying everywhere. It wasn't all bad, as I met a Medical Assistant there who became my wife. We are happily married and have three beautiful, intelligent and loving daughters.

Professionally, I have been involved with corporate documentation, training development and technology-based learning for most of my professional career. Along the way, I went back to school and got a Master's degree and later a Ph.D. in Education.

I have had a solid career working as an individual contributor and a manager. I have not held lofty positions nor am I wealthy, but I enjoy writing, using technology and trying to come up with creative ways to help people learn. However, the thing I am most proud of is being part of a loving family. When kids grow up in an environment that has mental and physical abuse, and deception, they sometimes repeat these same things with their families. I have not done that.

* * * *

What is the message you want this book to convey to readers?

Life outside of sports for me, or outside whatever your comfort zone is for you, is not always fluid.

Despite mixed results at times, through the years I have tried to follow these personal guidelines, which I had never formerly written down before authoring this book.

- **Build on the things you do well**—For me, it started with athletics. I did well in sports and enjoyed them. I tried just about all the sports available to me and usually had some level of success. This helped me gain confidence in my abilities and get involved with other people. As I grew older, I tried to apply the same approach in school and, eventually, work. It hasn't been as easy for me in these other areas, but gradually I have extended myself and become more comfortable and well-rounded.

- **Be persistent**—It is easy to do things that you like or are good at. It is not so easy to put yourself out there and leave yourself vulnerable to rejection or failure. There are still many times when I don't meet my own expectations, but I keep trying every day. I don't give up.

- **Be honest with yourself and don't make excuses**—It would be easy to blame others for my shortcomings or say that I got a bad deal as a child, but I try to accept responsibility for what I do and who I am. I also feel like this approach gives me control of my life. So when I achieve some level of success and meet my goals, it is satisfying. When I am not successful and admit my shortcomings, I think people respect that approach.

- **Be positive, not vindictive**—I am a glass half full type of person. I work hard to get what I want and I expect good things to happen. When they don't, I try not to dwell on the failures and unhappiness. I move on to the next thing and expect good results.

* * * *

Although I was a victim of Munchausen by Proxy, I was fortunate to survive and go on to live a good life. Others are not as fortunate. What could be done to detect and help children in these situations.

First of all, from what I understand, it is not common in today's world to put a young child in institutions for a prolonged period of time. Second, I do not want to position myself as an expert on MBP or child abuse; however, I can speak about my personal experience. Given those considerations, I think these approaches might help treating kids in a MBP situation:

- **Provider building rapport with the child or adolescent.** This connection can provide important support to the child and may allow the child to trust the provider and open up. I had a love of sports that was very important to me. My probation officer taking me to my first professional baseball game is something I will always remember, and helped me see him as someone who took an interest in me. The same could be said about the activities counselor who I played baseball with at the juvenile detention center. When the health care or other provider or teacher is seen by the patient or client as someone who goes beyond the mechanics of the job, that may open up opportunities to learn more about the youth. It may also allow the youth to appreciate that he or she is being cared for as a unique individual.

- **Ask direct questions that invite a direct answer, and promise confidentiality as far as the law allows.** I didn't fully understand what was going on with my mother, but I knew that things weren't entirely as she said they were. At the same time, I was afraid of my mother and did not want to anger her. In my earlier years dealing with the MBP situation, I am not sure what I would have shared if I was asked a direct question. However, as time went on, I think I would have answered direct questions about what my mother did to me, depending on who was asking and if I felt safe. As I got older and more aware of my mother's role in what was happening, I might have talked more freely in private to someone I trusted. The line of questioning could have built over time as I became more comfortable with the person inquiring.

- **Follow up with prior care providers to get a more complete family history**. Talking directly with the child's or adolescent's prior health care providers in a potential MBP situation might have provided insight into concerns that already existed and perhaps inconsistencies in medical history. My mother was often unhappy with my care, and frequently searched for the next physician or institution to begin all over again. Being aware of this pattern might have raised concerns beyond her immediate objections.

I offer these ideas as considerations if you are a health care or other provider and are faced with a perplexing situation in which MBP is possible.

16
Epilogue

Clement Chase was a successful businessman in Omaha, Nebraska, in the late 1800s. Progressive in his thinking, he encouraged his daughter, Carmelita, to explore her interests and not conform to the constraints often put on women at the time. Carmelita went on to attend Bryn Mawr College and studied to be a teacher, consistent with her love of learning and reading.

While working at the Hull House in Chicago, she met and married a lawyer named Sebastian Hinton. When Hinton was a child, his father had been a mathematician, interested in educating his kids about the three-dimensional X, Y and Z Cartesian coordinates. He built a structure that connected pieces of bamboo in a configuration that extended up, and side-to-side in all directions. Then he would call out three numbers and the kids had to figure what piece of the structure corresponded to these coordinates.

After marrying Sebastian, Carmelita opened a small nursery school. In 1920, enhancing his father's original design, Sebastian built and patented the first jungle gym for the school. In his paperwork to obtain a patent, Sebastian referenced the monkey instinct of climbing. It wasn't until the 1950s that the term monkey bars became a popular, alternative term for the playground equipment.

* * * *

My wife and I didn't get many chances to go away for the weekend when the kids were small, but we maintained an annual tradition, and went to one of the smaller Professional Golf Association (PGA) tournaments, just 50 miles away in Lufton. My wife had grown up watching golf on TV with her parents, and I had played the sport since I was a teenager, but the time away for us was more than the golf.

On Saturday, we usually hung around the hotel pool, read a book or a magazine, went to dinner and enjoyed each other. Then on Sunday, we went to the final day of the golf tournament. But this year was going to be a little different. On Saturday afternoon, we planned on trying to find Whitford Training Center, which was about 10-15 miles away from Lufton. I got the address for Whitford Training Center from one of my old post cards.

I didn't know if Whitford Training Center was still there, and I wasn't sure what I would remember and not remember. But with the realization about my mother's Munchausen by Proxy (MBP), I had a renewed interest in revisiting such an important place from my childhood. So, my wife had a map and her good sense of direction, and I had some strong and vague memories hovering in my head. We found Rt. 57 in Whitford. On the map, it looked like Pine Street, the address I had on my post cards, and Rt. 57 were the same road, at least for part of the way. Then we saw a large body of water on the right. That was the reservoir.

"That's where I caught a fish. Well, sort of. I got bored and abandoned my fishing rod, and a fish came along and bit my hook," I quipped.

As we drove along the road, I peered up at the hilly land.

"I think that might be it," I said. "No, that couldn't be it. Whitford Training Center had three levels of land and a brick building."

We continued to survey the buildings and grassy undulations until we were suddenly upon it.

"That's it," I exclaimed. "There's the hill we used to go sledding on."

We drove past the main gate, up the winding road and parked near the garages on the right.

We walked towards the entrance of the main building. It was closed and nobody seemed to be around. That was good. I didn't want to have to explain why I was there snooping around. We walked towards the back of the brick building. It looked like the place had been converted to offices, and a few signs indicated it was used by state employees. The metal grates were still in place, covering the windows. It gave me an eerie feeling. It really had been a prison for kids, including me.

I imagined Mr. Sullivan calling out, "Up and at 'em, move and strip 'em."

"One of those rooms was the laundry room, where we had to pick out what clothes we were going to wear for the week from a pile of clothes on the floor," I said, with a distance in time that made the story sound incredulous, but no longer emotional. "I always tried to get the white polo shirt to wear. That's why I always have one hanging in my closet."

The three flattened levels of land were still there, but masked by the dense pine trees, overgrown bushes and tall grass.

"There's the backstop where we played baseball. Mr. Kirk was my favorite counselor. He used to hit home runs almost every time he got up. The field seems a lot smaller than I remember it. And one of the counselors used to sing Moon River in a deep voice during the games. And this is where we had the 100-yard dash, but it looks like it is only 50 or 60 yards," I said.

"And one of the kids used to run so crazy. He'd twist his head side-to-side. He was so intense. He's the kid that stole my ribbon I won in the 100-yard dash. And he lied right to my face. He said he couldn't believe someone would steal my stuff when he was the one who did it."

EPILOGUE

We continued to walk across the baseball diamond to the out-field. And there it was, rising above the overgrown brush. The monkey bars, now old and rusty.

"I can't believe they're still here. I used to swing on the monkey bars and Mr. Kirk hit all those home runs over them. I wanted more than anything to catch one of his long hits, but I never did. None of the kids did," I marveled.

We took some pictures and walked around for a while longer. Coming back here was like visiting a museum and an old friend at the same time, as the structure stood the test of time and preserved memories of things I had buried decades ago. I was seven years old when I was admitted to Whitford Training Center as a Ward of the State and I was just a few weeks short of nine years old when I left to go home.

My life could have continued to go in wayward directions, with me bouncing in and out of institutions. Or perhaps I might have become violent like some of the delinquent kids I encountered, or maybe forever retreated to my own inner world.

A lot had transpired since that time. While I struggled to over-come low self-esteem and social awkwardness, I found comfort and confidence playing sports. With my persistence to make a fulfilling life for myself and later for my family, the ripple effect of those ef-forts had grown exponentially.

My wife and I walked across the baseball field and towards our car. This time, I was free to leave Whitford Training Center without approval from the Board.

* * * *

The End

References

Chapter 1
None

Chapter 2
"Battle of Borodino." Wikipedia, The Free Encyclopedia. http://en.wikipedia.org/wiki/Battle_of_Borodino
"1812 Overture." Wikipedia, The Free Encyclopedia. http://en.wikipedia.org/wiki/1812_overture

Chapter 3
"Mad Magazine Covers." Google Image Search. https://www.google.com/search?q=mad+magazine+covers&rlz=1C2KMZB_en US520US520&tbm=isch&tbo=u&source=univ&sa=X&ei=KVjdUsO LBoinsQSBv4DoBg&ved=0CDkQsAQ&biw=1520&bih=877#q=mad +magazine+covers+1961&tbm=isch&facrc=_&imgdii=_&imgrc=7 uZhg9PcbsszcM%253A%3Bz7HpI2jD9Uy6HM%3Bhttp%253A%25 2F%252Fwww.rankopedia.com%252FCandidatePix%252F66413. gif%3Bhttp%253A%252F%252Fwww.rankopedia. com%252FFavorite-MAD-Magazine-Cover(Subscription-Canceled) %252FStep2%252F19732%252F.htm%3B420%3B543

Chapter 4
"The Wizard of Oz (1939 Film). " Wikipedia, The Free Encyclopedia. http://en.wikipedia.org/wiki/The_Wizard_of_Oz_(1939_film)

Chapter 5
"Epilepsy." Wikipedia, The Free Encyclopedia. http://en.wikipedia.org/wiki/Epilepsy
Hippocrates, "On the Sacred Disease." Translated by Francis Adams. http://classics.mit.edu/Hippocrates/sacred.html

Chapter 6
None

Chapter 7
"Surviving Childhood Abuse." http://www.12stepforums.net/healingroom/surviving.html

Chapter 8
Rabbi Van Lanckton. "New England States Punished "Stubborn Children" Under Laws Based On Deuteronomy, In Disregard Of Talmudic Commentary Abrogating Any Such Punishment." http://ravalsruminations.blogspot.com/2011/11/new-england-states-punished-stubborn.html
"Henry Bergh." Wikipedia, The Free Encyclopedia. http://en.wikipedia.org/wiki/Henry_Bergh

Chapter 9
http://www.ehow.com/about_6598999_history-juvenile-detention-center.html
http://www.cjcj.org/Education1/Juvenile-Justice-History.html
http://www.sagepub.com/hanserintro/study/materials/reference/ref13.2.pdf

Chapter 10
"Harmon Killebrew." Wikipedia, The Free Encyclopedia. http://en.wikipedia.org/wiki/Harmon_Killebrew

Chapter 11
"A Brief History of Snow Sledding in Europe." http://www.alpinesleds.com/sledding-history.html
"Flexible Flyer." Wikipedia, The Free Encyclopedia. http://en.wikipedia.org/wiki/Flexible_flyer

Chapter 12
"The History of Postcards." http://www.emotionscards.com/museum/historyofpostcards.htm
"Postcard." Wikipedia, The Free Encyclopedia. http://en.wikipedia.org/wiki/Postcard

Chapter 13
"John Augustus." Wikipedia, The Free Encyclopedia. http://en.wikipedia.org/wiki/John_augustus Baseball Reference.com.
"Bill Monbouquette." http://www.baseball-reference.com/players/m/monbobi01.shtml
Baseball Reference.com. "Thursday July 22, 1965 Fenway Park." http://www.baseball-reference.com/boxes/BOS/BOS196507220.shtml
"List of Major League No-hitters." Wikipedia, The Free Encyclopedia. http://en.wikipedia.org/wiki/List_of_Major_League_Baseball_no-hitters
"Medford's Bill Monbouquette Celebrates Golden Anniversary of No-hitter." http://www.wickedlocal.com/medford/news/x246334832/Medfords-Bill-Monbouquette-celebrates-golden-anniversary-of-no-hitter
"Former Red Sox Pitcher Bill Monbouquette Fought, Beat Cancer

With Help of Jimmy Fund (Video)." http://nesn.com/2013/08/
former-red-sox-pitcher-bill-monbouquette-fought-beat-cancer-
with-help-of-jimmy-fund-video/

Chapter 14
"Child Abuse." Wikipedia, The Free Encyclopedia. http://
en.wikipedia.org/wiki/Child_abuse
"National Child Abuse Statistics: Child Abuse in America." http://
www.childhelp-usa.com/pages/statistics

Chapter 15
"Munchausen Syndrome by Proxy." Wikipedia,
The Free Encyclopedia. http://en.wikipedia.org/
wiki/M%C3%BCnchausen_syndrome_by_proxy
Feldman, Marc D. and Ford, Charles V., <u>Patient or Pretender:
Inside the Strange World of Factitious Disorders</u>. John Wiley &
Sons, New York, NY. 1994.

Chapter 16
None